Organic
Farming

About the Authors

Stephan Dabbert is Professor of Agricultural and Resource Economics and in October 2002 became Dean of the Faculty of Agriculture, at the University of Hohenheim in Stuttgart, Germany. He was co-ordinator of the EU-funded project 'Organic Farming and the CAP' which was a major effort to analyse organic farming policy within the European Union, Switzerland and Norway. He acts as an adviser to the EU Commission and the German Federal Government on organic farming policy issues, and has published widely in the area of organic farming, agri-environmental policy and water protection. He is the editor of the book series *Organic Farming in Europe: Economics and Policy*.

Anna Maria Häring is a researcher at the Institute of Farm Economics at the University of Hohenheim in Stuttgart, Germany. She participated in the interdisciplinary EU Project 'Organic Farming and the Common Agricultural Policy'. Her PhD was on the relationship between EU agricultural policy, farm economics and organic farming. She has published many articles and contributed to several books.

Raffaele Zanoli is Professor of Agro-Food Marketing at the Polytechnic University of Marche, Italy. He is currently president of the Italian Research Group in Organic Farming (GRAB-IT) and has participated in many EU-funded research projects on organic farming. In 1996 he was appointed Coordinator of the FAO Working Group on Research Methodologies in Organic Farming. He has published over a hundred articles on agricultural economics, marketing and policy.

The authors continue their collaboration as partners in the EU-funded project 'Further Development of Organic Farming Policy in Europe with Particular Emphasis on EU Enlargement'.

Organic Farming

POLICIES AND PROSPECTS

Stephan Dabbert

Anna Maria Häring

Raffaele Zanoli

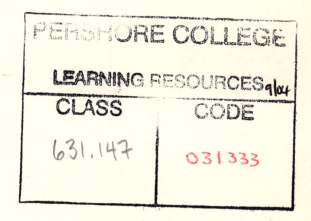

Zed Books

LONDON & NEW YORK

Organic Farming: Policies and Prospects was first published by
Zed Books Ltd, 7 Cynthia Street, London N1 9JF, UK and
Room 400, 175 Fifth Avenue, New York, NY 10010, USA, in 2004

www.zedbooks.co.uk

Cover designed by Andrew Corbett
Typeset in 10.6/13 pt Goudy by Long House, Cumbria, UK
Printed and bound in the United Kingdom
by Biddles Ltd, Guildford and King's Lynn

Distributed in the USA exclusively by Palgrave Macmillan, a division of
St Martin's Press, LLC,175 Fifth Avenue, New York, NY 10010

A catalogue record for this book is available from the British Library
Library of Congress Cataloging-in-Publication Data is available

ISBN   Hb 1 84277 326 7 (Zed Books)
        Pb 1 84277 327 5 (Zed Books)

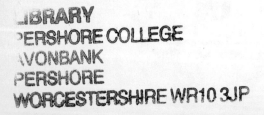

Contents

List of Boxes

List of Tables

List of Figures

Glossary

ACQUIS COMMUNAUTAIRE: The entire body of European laws is known as the *acquis communautaire*. This includes all the treaties, regulations and directives passed by the European institutions as well as judgements laid down by the Court of Justice. The term is most often used in connection with preparations by the 12 candidate countries to join the union. They must adopt, implement and enforce all the *acquis* to be allowed to join the European Union (EU).

AGRIBUSINESS: Includes all the activities that take place in the production, manufacturing, distribution, wholesale and retail sales of an agricultural commodity.

ALTERNATIVE FARMING: Non-conventional, but not necessarily organic farming – although often used as a synonym for the latter.

CAIRNS GROUP: A group formed in 1986 in Cairns, Australia. The group seeks the removal of trade barriers and substantial reductions in subsidies affecting agricultural trade in response to depressed commodity prices and reduced export earnings stemming from subsidy wars between the United States (US) and the EU. Its members account for a significant portion of the world's agricultural exports and include major food exporters from both developed and developing countries: Argentina, Australia, Bolivia, Brazil, Canada, Chile, Colombia, Costa Rica, Fiji, Guatemala, Indonesia, Malaysia, New Zealand, Paraguay, the Philippines, Thailand, South Africa and Uruguay. The Cairns Group was a strong coalition in the Uruguay Round of multilateral trade negotiations under the General Agreement on Tariffs and Trade (GATT).

CODEX ALIMENTARIUS: A set of standards on maximum chemical residues in food devised by a committee established by the Food and Agriculture

Organisation (FAO) and the World Health Organisation (WHO).

CONSUMER PROTECTION: Consumer protection laws are statutes governing sales and credit practices involving consumer goods. Such statutes prohibit and regulate deceptive or unscrupulous advertising and sales practices, product quality, credit financing and reporting, debt collection, leases, and other aspects of consumer transactions. The goal of consumer protection laws is to place consumers, who are average citizens engaging in business deals such as buying goods or borrowing money, on an even par with companies or citizens who regularly engage in business.

EXPORT SUBSIDIES: Special incentives provided by governments to encourage increased foreign sales. Subsidies, which are contingent on export performance, may take the form of cash payments, disposal of government stocks at below-market prices, subsidies financed by producers or processers as a result of government actions such as assessments, marketing subsidies, transportation and freight subsidies, and subsidies for commodities contingent on their incorporation in exported products.

INTEGRATED FARMING: A farming system that aims to reduce the environmental impact of agriculture while pursuing economic goals. Standards are voluntary. The farming system is not legally certified.

MARKET FAILURE: The failure of the market to include in the price of a good the costs or benefits of an externality (a harmful or beneficial side-effect that occurs in the production, consumption or distribution of a particular good). Often, government policies in the form of regulations (such as standards, bans and restrictions on input use) and incentive-based mechanisms (such as taxes, subsidies and marketable permits) are implemented as corrective measures (Henrichsmeyer and Witzke: 58).

MARKET DISTORTION: Factors (such as taxes, subsidies or quotas) that cause the market price and quantity for a given good or service to differ from the equilibrium level.

MARKET NON-TRANSPARENCY: A lack of market overview. The setting of a uniform price is hampered, as is the ability of producers to adapt to changed market conditions.

MULTIFUNCTIONALITY: The EU tries to define agriculture as multifunctional, as more than the production of food and fibre. Multifunctionality recognises the principles of sustainability. In this view, agriculture also has economic, ecological, social, cultural and other functions.

NON-RENEWABLE RESOURCES: A natural resource, such as fossil fuels, that has a finite stock and cannot be renewed.

ORGANIC FARMING: A set of agricultural practices in which no artificial fertilisers, hormones, pesticides or herbicides are used. Organic farming is increasingly popular in developed countries as consumers become more concerned over the potential health hazards of chemical residues in food. Boxes 1.1 and 1.2 (pp. 3–5) provide a more detailed definition.

POLICY INTERVENTION: Any politically motivated intervention to develop the economy. Interventions in the agricultural sector are usually aimed at harmonising supply and demand.

PRECAUTIONARY PRINCIPLE: This advocates action – such as banning the import of genetically modified organisms – when the safety of products cannot be established with full scientific certainty and potentially hazardous consequences in the future are suspected.

PRICE PREMIUM: The extra money received by farmers or paid by consumers for a quality/premium product.

PRIVATE GOOD: A good, such as an automobile, used and enjoyed exclusively by its owner.

PUBLIC GOOD: A good, such as air or national defence, that cannot practicably be denied to any individual without denying it to everyone; that continues to be available regardless of how much a given individual consumes; and that therefore must be produced or regulated by government action, rather than by the marketplace, in order to ensure socially optimal availability.

SUBSIDIARITY: Principle, specified in the EU Common Act (Article 5), by which governmental or societal responsibilities are assumed by the smallest possible administrative unit.

SUSTAINABLE AGRICULTURE: Methods of farming that do not degrade the productive capacity of the land.

WELFARE THEORY: A macroeconomic discipline theory, dealing with the most efficient allocation of resources in an economy. An important aspect of welfare theory is the so-called Pareto criterion.

Abbreviations

€	Euro
AIR	Third EU research framework
AWU	Agricultural work unit
BSE	Bovine Spongiform Encephalopathy
CA	Codex Alimentarius
CAP	Common Agricultural Policy
CEE	Central and Eastern European countries
CH_4	Methane
CO_2	Carbon dioxide
DARCOF	Danish Research Centre for Organic Farming
EFRC	Elm Farm Research Centre
EU	European Union
FAIR	Fourth EU research framework
FAL	Bundesforschungsanstalt für Landwirtschaft
FAO	Food and Agriculture Organisation
FCM	Fat corrected milk
FDB	Danish Cooperative Retail and Wholesale Society
FiBL	Forschungsinstitut für biologischen Landbau
FMD	Foot and Mouth Disease
GATT	General Agreement on Tariffs and Trade
GMO	Genetically modified organism
ha	Hectare(s)

HDRA	Henry Doubleday Research Association
IFOAM	International Federation of Organic Agriculture Movements
IOAS	International Organic Accreditation Service
ITC	International Trade Centre
K	Potassium
kg	Kilogram
LU	Livestock unit
N	Nitrogen
N_2O	Nitrous oxide
NGO	Non-governmental organisation
NH_3	Ammonia
NUTS	Nomenclature Unités Territoriales Statistiques
OCIS	Organic Conversion Information Service (UK)
OF	Organic farming
ÖPZ	Öko-Prüfzeichen
P	Potassium
UAA	Utilisable agricultural area
UK	United Kingdom
US	United States
USDA	United States Department of Agriculture
VAT	Value added tax
WHO	World Health Organisation
WTO	World Trade Organisation
WWF	World Wildlife Fund

Acknowledgements

The work underlying this publication has been carried out with financial support from the Commission of the European Communities, Agriculture and Fisheries (FAIR) Research and Technology Development (RTD) programme, project FAIR3-CT96-1794, 'Effects of the CAP-reform and possible further developments of organic farming in the EU'. The authors are grateful for this support.

The project brought together a group of scientists and practitioners from 18 European countries. This report is largely based on their work. Special thanks go to project partners Carolyn Foster, Danilo Gambelli, Nic Lampkin, Kennet Lynggaard, Johannes Michelsen, Peter Midmore, Hiltrud Nieberg, Frank Offermann, Susanne Padel, Mathias Stolze, and Daniela Vairo.

The authors also wish to express their gratitude to the co-authors of selected project reports: Ulrich Hamm, Annette Piorr, Eva Roth and Els Wynen are thanked.

Without the contribution of numerous subcontractors in the project this publication could not have been produced.

Our appreciation also goes to Hillary Crowe for proofreading the final document.

This publication does not necessarily reflect the European Commission's views and in no way anticipates the Commission's future policy in this area. Its content is the sole responsibility of the authors.

Preface

The growing public debate on organic farming and its position in the policy environment is often dominated by prejudice rather than facts, a situation partly due to a lack of comprehensive information on the topic. A wide range of studies is available on more detailed questions, but an incisive overview is hard to find.

What can our readers expect from the following pages? We try to provide answers to the following questions:

1 What is the state of organic farming in Europe at the start of the new millennium, and how did the sector evolve?

2 What are the potential benefits of organic farming for society and how can these benefits be taken into consideration in shaping agricultural policy?

3 How will the general policy environment change in the future and how will this affect organic farming?

4 What is the best way to include organic farming in the European policy environment?

In answering these questions we attempt to balance criticism of and sympathy with organic farming, and to highlight its strengths and weaknesses. While we aim to challenge uncritical preconceptions wherever possible, we do not deny our positive attitude towards organic farming.

We consider organic farming as part of a more comprehensive agricultural policy. Nevertheless, this book concentrates on organic farming and inevitably factors out much information on the main agricultural sectors and many elements of agricultural policy.

Reflecting the availability of data, examples and background information refer mainly to the European Union. Conclusions and recommendations on organic farming policy nevertheless have a much wider application.

For the general reader a glossary of terms is provided (pp. x–xii). Numerous boxes (see List of Boxes, p. vii) provide additional information. We wish you fruitful reading.

Stephan Dabbert, Anna Maria Häring and Raffaele Zanoli

CHAPTER 1

Organic farming: grassroots movement or policy directive?

In the twentieth century we have witnessed dramatic technological changes in agriculture which have completely transformed the rural landscape and the habits of rural populations. The key element of this technological revolution, which still continues in many parts of the world today, was the substitution of on-farm by off-farm resources. It became economically profitable to replace farm labour with machinery, and soil fertility could easily be enhanced by buying chemical fertilisers. This reduces the use of farming systems which rely on the internal preservation and production of soil fertility. The invention of a variety of chemical pesticides allowed harvests to be protected from pests and led, at the same time, to simplified agricultural systems that were based on regular applications of these pesticides while abandoning various prophylactic non-chemical measures that were formerly an integral part of farming. The tendency to detach agriculture from its natural roots, which was inherent in these technological developments, became especially visible in some forms of animal husbandry, such as the housing of laying hens in batteries where they are completely separated from anything that might resemble a natural environment.

In the industrialised countries like those of Western Europe, where these developments are especially strong, a number of key advantages were associated with the new forms of agriculture. Labour and soil productivity increased and food became abundant and cheap for the consumer. The labour force that left agriculture could be productive in other areas of society and thus increase total wealth.

However, there are also a number of major problems associated with these developments. In many cases modern agricultural technologies had a very negative impact on the natural environment, with a massive build-up of nutrient surpluses in some regions and intensive use of pesticides in others. Animal welfare became a major issue in societies, not only because of the advent of methods of animal rearing that closely resemble industrial production but also because the more affluent societies became very concerned about animal welfare. The loss of heritage landscapes and biodiversity, which in many cases had been created by earlier forms of agriculture and were now being destroyed by modern forms, became further areas of concern. The decline of the agricultural population in rural areas meant major structural change and was often accompanied by above-average unemployment rates and difficult social conditions in formerly agricultural regions.

Organic agriculture is a system that had been developed in Europe long before the impact of the major technological revolution in agriculture, described above, became obvious. Its pioneers' idea was to develop the farm as a system which makes use of its own resources as far as possible and only draws on external resources when necessary and appropriate. The key idea of organic farming is to use modern technology selectively and avoid those elements which are inherently risky or environmentally damaging, or which might lead to the separation of farming from its natural environment. This idea was developed largely outside the agricultural research establishment and went largely unnoticed by the public for decades.

In Europe, organic farming underwent dynamic development during the last decade of the twentieth century. In the European Union (EU), the organically farmed area increased five-fold from 1993 to 2000 (Lampkin 2002), and the concept of organic farming is becoming increasingly familiar to the general public. Not only are consumers more aware of organic products, but policies which influence organic farming have also become a key element in the toolbox of agricultural policy makers.

In this book, we generally take the EU as our region of reference. The reason for this is simple: in terms of organic farming policy, the EU leads the world. European regulations on organic farming have exercised a strong influence on the development of rules in other parts of the world. Support policies have now been in place for 15 years, and the European organic farming regime came ten years before equivalent US legislation, which was only implemented in 2002. So we believe that there is much to learn from this wealth of experience with organic farming policy. It is obvious that some of the lessons learned from highly industrialised Western Europe (the 15 member states of the EU) are most useful for other industrialised countries with high income levels and a commitment to a proactive agricultural policy. However, with EU enlargement, these policies will also become relevant for new member states with a very different history of agricultural development. We thus believe that the ideas and policies we discuss have obvious relevance beyond the EU in its current form. We do not explore in any depth the potential contribution of organic farming to improving productivity in countries and regions where external inputs are hard to obtain and where self-sufficiency and subsistence are important, an issue which has recently been covered in more depth by the Food and Agriculture Organisation (FAO) (2002).

Agricultural policy provides the regulatory framework for all economic and political measures designed to influence the agribusiness sector. The nature of these interventions has a significant impact on the development of agribusiness. The first Europe-wide policy intervention in organic farming is as recent as the beginning of the 1990s. A state-supervised certification system for organic products was established (Council Regulation 2092/91) (EC 1991) and subsidies for organic production were introduced. For the first time, a formal system of certification guaranteed to the consumer that products labelled as organic had genuinely been produced organically. The EU definition of organic farming involves holistic production systems for crops and livestock based, where possible, on cultural, biological and mechanical methods instead of synthetic materials. A more detailed description is given by the Codex Alimentarius (CA) adopted by the FAO (see Box 1.1).

Box 1.1   What is organic farming? (CAC 2001)

Organic agriculture is based on holistic production management systems which promote and enhance agro-ecosystem health, including bio-diversity, biological cycles, and soil biological activity. It emphasises the use of management practices in preference to the use of off-farm inputs, taking into account that regional conditions require locally adapted systems. This is accomplished by using, where possible, cultural, biological and mechanical methods, as opposed to synthetic materials, to fulfil any specific function within the system. An organic production system is designed to:

a) Enhance biological diversity within the whole system;

b) Increase soil biological activity;

➡

c) Maintain long-term soil fertility;

d) Recycle wastes of plant and animal origin in order to return nutrients to the land, thus minimising the use of non-renewable resources;

e) Rely on renewable resources in locally organised agricultural systems;

f) Promote the healthy use of soil, water and air as well as minimising all forms of pollution that may result from agricultural practices;

g) Handle agricultural products with emphasis on careful processing methods in order to maintain the organic integrity and vital qualities of the product at all stages;

h) Become established on any existing farm through a period of conversion, the appropriate length of which is determined by site-specific factors such as the history of the land and the type of crops and livestock to be produced.

Of course, these government measures were not the beginning of organic farming. Organic farming dates back to the first quarter of the twentieth century – before the widespread use of synthetic pesticides and soluble nitrogen fertilisers which has characterised agriculture over the last five decades. The basic philosophy of organic farming has been around since the start of the twentieth century. Box 1.2 gives an impression of how broadly the concept of organic farming is defined. Equally broad is the range of terms used. We prefer the use of organic farming which is, however, synonymous with ecological, biological, eco- or bio-farming.

In the 1970s, organic farming managed to raise sympathies within the environmental movement. These were translated into a desire to give political support to organic farming and paved the way for the growth in demand for organic products in later years. Until the 1980s, however, organic farming was a social movement which defined itself as being 'in opposition' not only to conventional farming but also to much of the institutional setting of agriculture in general, with regard to both education and policy making. Similarly, the established institutions tended to

---

Box 1.2 Philosophy of organic farming (Lampkin *et al*. 1999a)

Organic farming can be seen as an approach to agriculture where the aim is to create integrated, humane, environmentally and economically sustainable agricultural production systems. The term 'organic' is best thought of as referring not to the type of inputs used, but to the concept of the farm as an organism, in which all the components — the soil minerals, organic matter, microorganisms, insects, plants, animals and humans — interact to create a coherent, self-regulating and stable whole. Reliance on external inputs, whether chemical or organic, is reduced as far as possible. In many European countries, organic agriculture is known as ecological or biological agriculture, reflecting the reliance on ecosystem management rather than external inputs.

---

ignore the existence of organic farming or viewed it as a backward technology practised by a tiny 'lunatic fringe'.

This situation changed completely at the end of the 1980s and the beginning of the 1990s as a result of two developments. At that time, the absence of a clear legal framework meant that conventional products could be sold to the consumer as 'organic', and terms such as natural, ecological or biological could be used for conventional products. This market non-transparency and lack of consumer protection justified political action.

Second, the environmental movement gained considerable political influence during the 1980s. Although the environmental movement and the organic farming movement were not identical in terms of organisation and objectives, growing public interest in environmental matters led to greater sympathy for organic farming which translated into a desire to give it political support for environmental reasons.

It was the first of these developments that led to an attempt to standardise what was meant by organic farming and – most importantly – what was meant by 'organic food'. The second development led to the introduction of support programmes in some countries (Denmark, Germany) in the late 1980s and in the EU as part of the 1992 Common Agricultural Policy (CAP) reform.

From the organic movement's perspective, this formal political recognition was a landmark in the development of organic farming in Europe. Organic farming suddenly became an agricultural policy instrument – after being 'in opposition' to the agricultural policy establishment for many years. The power to define the concept of organic farming has shifted as well. Today, the question 'What is organic farming?' is defined legally by institutions like the EU that were opposed to organic farming for decades. However, this only holds true for the minimum definition. The organic sector still strongly influences this minimum definition and can establish stricter rules above this legal minimum through the private standards and regulations set by the organic farming organisations. Within the organic movement, the shift towards an institutionalised definition of the basic concept has sparked considerable protest.

For policy makers, defining this concept was a new sphere of action and several difficulties resulted, especially because the organic farming movements in different countries were not unified in their approaches to practical details, despite agreement on principles. While organic farming had always centred on the key concept of 'the farm as a closed system', the European regulation which defined the term in 1991 referred only to plant production and thus left an important part of organic farming outside its definition. Having organic plant production but conventional animal production conflicts with organic principles. In many member states standards on animal production already existed, but very different structural, climatic and cultural conditions meant that many years passed before a commonly accepted framework for organic animal production could be agreed. In 1999 the European regulation on animal production in organic farming came into effect, after nearly a decade of working with a definition that was a mere shadow of the original concept of organic farming.

Today, in the view of some observers, policy is acquiring greater influence on the organic farming sector than the organic farming movement itself. This development was probably inevitable for a number of reasons:

- The EU policy-framing bodies are organised in a more centralised way. The power to define organic farming lies in the hands of one organisation and the resulting definition of organic farming is binding on an EU-wide level. In contrast, the organic farming movement is made up of a wide range of producer organisations, certifying bodies, etcetera. In some countries, there may even be a number of interest groups or organisations. Little imagination is required to picture the organisational power of a social movement compared with an official policy organisation.

- Policy makers are becoming more aware of the basic concepts of organic farming and the development and characteristics of the organic food market, not least because administrations at all levels became more deeply involved with organic farming during the last decade of the twentieth century.

As a result, the organic movement has begun to recognise the need to respond to this policy influence. Closer cooperation with official bodies is increasingly considered an integral part of lobbying strategy. Given the oppositional nature of the social movement during its early stages, co-operation with the agricultural establishment was not high on the agenda, and communication was poor. This lack of communication was probably the reason why so much policy making was based on ignorance (Michelsen et al. 2001).

Although policy is gaining influence over the legal definition of organic farming in the EU, the International Federation of Organic Agriculture Movements (IFOAM) is a leader in this debate. A key question is how to define a broader, more holistic concept of organic farming that also sets minimum social standards for the people involved in organic farming.

The public debate on organic farming centres around the justification of the system in comparison with conventional or other alternative farming systems. A distinction between organic farming and other alternative farming systems – such as integrated farming – is seen in the existence of detailed production standards and certification procedures (IFOAM 1996, for example) to draw a clear dividing line. In contrast to other sustainable farming systems, this allows the use of the market to support the environmental, social and animal welfare objectives (Lampkin et al. 1999a).

The arguments most commonly used in favour of organic farming are its potential contribution to society's needs, such as safe food and a clean environment. Opponents of organic farming consider it a farming system preferred by romantics who stick to a nineteenth-century approach to agriculture without seeing that the world has changed. Several arguments are related to the lower yields in organic agriculture due to the rejection of external inputs. Critics are concerned about the ability of organic farming to produce sufficient food for everyone, the necessity of increasing imports, the high prices of organic food and potential fraud. Moreover, these critics doubt whether the quality of organic food is any different and whether the environmental effects are indeed less detrimental than those of other farming systems.

Organic farming has become a key instrument in policy-making tool-boxes over the last decade. It is therefore worth reflecting on the various aspects of organic farming and how it can be treated by policy makers. This book is intended to provide a sound base for a fruitful dialogue between non-governmental organisations (NGOs, such as the organic farming organisations) and governmental policy makers on the development of organic farming policy.

CHAPTER 2

Organic farming in Europe at the dawn of the new millennium

Organic farming is practised in nearly all countries of the world, and a growing number of farms occupy an expanding land area. In total, some 17 million hectares of land are cultivated organically worldwide (Willer and Yussefi 2002). Of these, 45 per cent are located in Oceania (mainly Australia), 25 per cent in Europe and 22 per cent in Latin America (Willer and Yussefi 2002). In North America, nearly 1.3 million hectares are farmed organically. The highest share of total agricultural land area – more than 3 per cent – is observed in the European Union (Lampkin 2002).

Markets for organic products are growing rapidly within and beyond North America, Japan and Europe (Kortbech-Olesen 2002). Although organic farming was established in many other countries in response to growing demand in these three regions, domestic markets are now developing as well. Governments and international organisations are increasingly supporting organic farming.

Farms, land area and regional distribution

Organic farms and land area

Within European agriculture, organic farming is the exception. In contrast to other parts of agriculture, organic farming is a growth sector (Figure 2.1). The dynamic development observed in the last decade of the twentieth century offers an opportunity to reflect on future trends in organic farming in Europe. Will the organic farming sector continue to grow at a similar rate? Or has its maximum development taken place? Will it now stagnate at the current level?

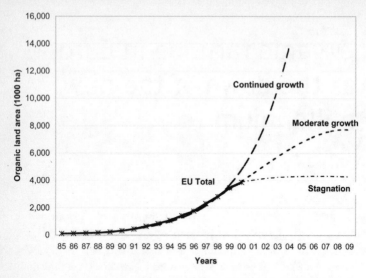

Figure 2.1 **The development of organic farming in the European Union** (forecasts based on Foster and Lampkin 2000)

Most people involved in agriculture would probably answer that the likely future trend for organic farming is continued growth, eventually levelling off to a state of equilibrium. It is also possible that the growth phase of organic farming is already over and that the organic land area will stagnate in the future.

Although rapid growth has been observed in absolute terms, the organic farming sector is still quite small, covering only about 3 per cent of total agricultural land area in the EU. The aggregated figures for the EU as a whole mask vast differences in countries, regions and farm types.

In terms of land area, Italy has by far the largest organic sector in Europe, followed by Germany, the UK, Spain and France (Figure 2.2). Although the organic farming sector is quite large, in relative terms, in Sweden, Austria, Denmark, Finland and Switzerland, they have substantially less organic land area in absolute terms.

Regional distribution
One interesting question to ask is why organic farming is spread so unevenly throughout Europe, something which becomes especially apparent if we look at the regional distribution of organic farming (Figure 2.3). Apart from

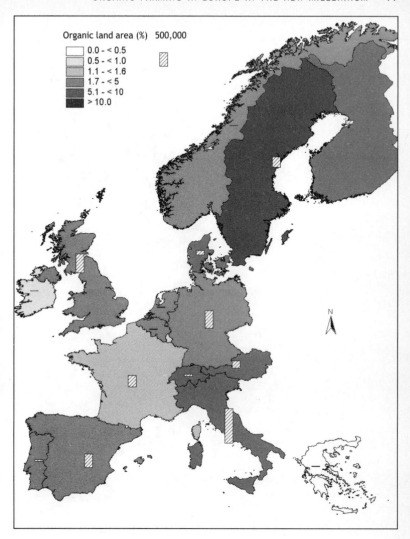

Figure 2.2   The distribution of the organically farmed area in Europe in 2000 (Bichler and Schuster 2002, based on Eurostat 2002)

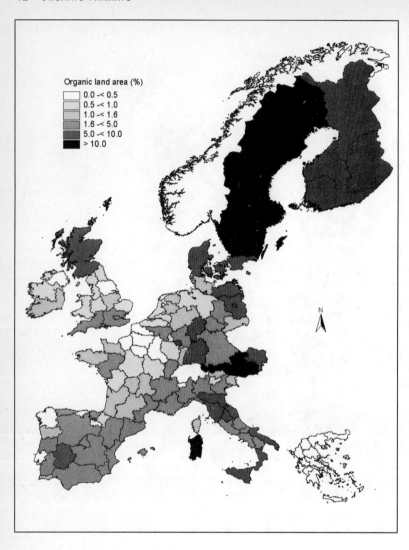

**Figure 2.3   Regional distribution of organic and in-conversion land
area in Europe in 2000**

(Bichler and Schuster 2002, based on Eurostat 2002)

the quality of soils, the level of intensity and specialisation of agricultural practices and the influence of general agricultural policy are possible explanations. The leading countries in the development of organic farming (in terms of the percentage of organic to total land area) have most certainly experienced strong policy support for organic farming. In most cases, this has included special support for the markets for organic foodstuffs. However, if the distribution of organic land within a country or a region with a uniform policy regime is uneven, other reasons must prevail. Two arguments which immediately come to mind are the quality of soils and climate and – given the importance of direct marketing in organic farming compared to conventional farming in the early development stages – the proximity of the farms to cities.

In some countries – Germany, Austria and Switzerland – organic farming is much more likely to be found in disadvantaged rural areas where extensive agriculture predominates (Dabbert and Braun 1993; Osterburg *et al.* 1997; Hartnagel 1998; Schneeberger *et al.* 1997). What is the logic behind this simple observation? In disadvantaged regions, conventional agriculture is usually organised quite differently from conventional agriculture in intensive regions. Grasslands tend to be more important than arable land, and less fertiliser is used on agricultural lands. Extensive forms of animal production such as beef/dairy cattle or sheep tend to play the major role in these regions, whereas intensive animal production systems such as poultry or pig production are rarely found.

If a conventional farmer relies heavily on feedstuffs, especially roughage, produced on his own farm to feed his animals, and low amounts of pesticides and synthetic fertilisers are used, the changes the farm has to undergo to convert to organic agriculture tend to be small. Even if no additional price premium for organic produce is received and no policy-related payments are made for organic farming, the loss a farmer undergoes when converting to organic agriculture is fairly small. If, in such a situation, price premiums can be achieved or agri-environmental payments are made for being organic, organic farming tends to be more profitable than conventional farming. If, on the other hand, a conventional farm relies on highly intensive animal rearing, such as poultry, a conversion to organic farming requires major changes in the organisation of the farm. In that case, the number of animals has to be drastically reduced because the organic production standards do not allow the purchase of large amounts of feedstuffs necessary to sustain the original level of production. The method of animal rearing must also be altered radically because some cost-efficient methods,

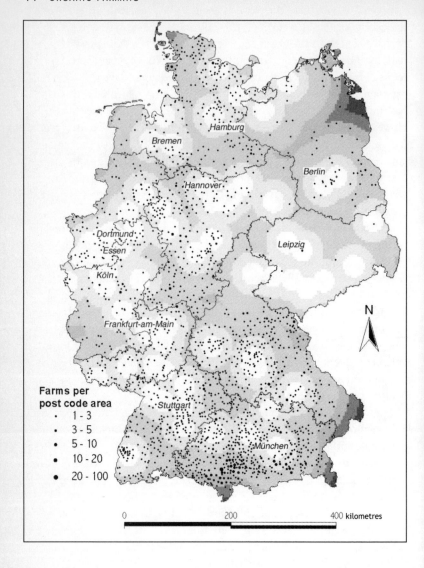

Figure 2.4 **Germany: regional distribution of organic farms (Bioland) and their distance from large cities** (Mövius *et al.* 1998)

such as battery farming of hens, cannot be used in organic farming. Specialist conventional arable producers use a large part of their land for production of a few cash crops and would need to introduce fertility-building crops into their rotation in order to farm organically. It is obvious that this requirement could lead to drastic decreases in income.

An attempt to test this argument on a European level has been made by Offermann (2000a), who found that within countries or regional clusters with similar conditions, relatively high shares of organic farms are most likely to be found in regions unfavourable to agricultural production.

Considering the importance of direct marketing in the early stages of development of organic farming, it seems logical to ask whether proximity to the consumers explains this uneven spatial distribution. The example of one organic farming association in Germany (Bioland) shows that this has no direct influence (Figure 2.4) (Mövius *et al.* 1998). Within the regions with high numbers of organic farms, the concentration of farms close to cities was no higher than elsewhere.

Incidental events may also contribute to the development of organic farming in a region or country, helping to overcome the high costs of establishment of organic farming, as incurred for example in the provision of infrastructure or information. Such events and an accumulation of expert knowledge may help to further develop the sector. Again, this may result in positive network externalities in technology and the exchange of

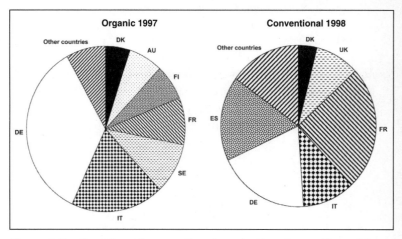

Figure 2.5   Organic and conventional production shares (% area) in Europe (Offermann 2000)

information (Latacz-Lohmann *et al.* 2001). Although several factors are suggested, for the time being we must conclude that the factors determining the regional distribution of organic farming are not yet fully understood.

Interestingly, this uneven spatial distribution of organic farming within Europe also has an effect on the regional distribution of production (Figure 2.5). For example, more than one third of all organic cereals produced in the EU is grown in Germany. In contrast, the largest producer of conventional cereals – France – only produces 9 per cent of the EU's organic cereals. The regional volumes of organic cereal production depend largely on the regional shares of arable land, the relative importance of single crops, and yield levels (Offermann 2000). In the example mentioned, France, the small size of the organic sector accounts for some of the observed differences.

Summary
Organic farming was a rapidly growing sub-sector of European agriculture during the last decade of the twentieth century. A smooth growth curve at European level masks markedly distinct developments in single countries. The overall significance of organic farming in the European context is still quite small in terms of land area used. Although organic farms tend to be found in the least profitable areas for agriculture, the uneven spatial distribution of organic farming is not yet fully understood. A concentration of organic farms in less favourable regions may be due to economic factors. As a consequence of this uneven spatial distribution across Europe, some important countries in terms of conventional cereal production (like France and Spain) do not rank very high on the list in organic production, mainly because of their small organic sectors. Their place is taken by countries which rank much lower in conventional cereal production but are characterised by a higher share of organic farming. Policy and market influences are likely factors explaining why organic farming is much more important in some countries than in others.

Markets

Size, growth, *per capita* spending
As a proportion of the total food market, the market for organic food and beverages is still quite small (Table 2.1). In absolute terms, retail sales are substantial and are estimated to stand at around US$17.5 billion for the

most important countries. In the medium term, further growth in retail sales is expected at a rate of 10–30 per cent per year. However, the largest markets in 2000 are not necessarily expected to grow at the fastest rate, whereas other minor markets are expected to expand rapidly.

Table 2.1   World markets for organic food and beverages: overview 2000[1] (ITC 2001)

Markets	Organic retail sales (US$ million)	Organic retail sales (%) of total food sales	Expected medium-term annual growth rate (%)
Germany	2,200–2,400	1.2–1.5	10–15
UK	1,000–1,050	1.0	25–30
Italy	1,000–1,050	1.0	15–20
France	750–800	1.0	15–20
Switzerland	425–450	2.0–2.5	15–20
Denmark	350–375	2.5–3.0	10–15
Austria	250–300	2.0	10–15
Netherlands	225–275	0.7–1.0	10–20
Sweden	125–150	1.0	20–25
Other Europe[2]	300–400	–	–
Subtotal (Europe)	7,000	–	–
USA	8,000	1.5	15–20
Japan	2,500	–	–
Total approx.	17,500	–	–

[1] Estimates; official trade statistics are not available. The figures for Japan are particularly uncertain, as they also include non-certified products classed as 'green'.
[2] Belgium, Finland, Greece, Ireland, Portugal, Spain, Norway

Germany, for example, the largest market within Europe, is expected to continue to grow at 10–15 per cent, which would amount to a yearly increase in retail sales volume of approximately US$340 million. Similar annual growth in retail sales of organic food of approximately US$300 million (25–30 per cent annual growth) is expected in the UK, starting from a mere 1 per cent market share of total food sales in 2000. In contrast, in Denmark, organic food has accounted for a substantial share – nearly 3 per cent – of the total retail volume for some time. Nonetheless, the expected growth rate of 10–15 per cent per year would only amount to an approximate annual increase in retail sales of US$50 million.

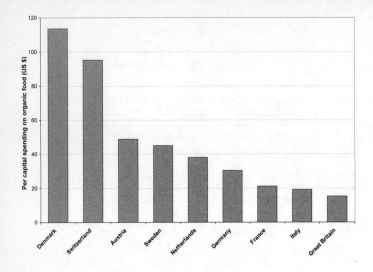

Figure 2.6 **Estimated *per capita* spending on organic foods in 2000 by country** (Yussefi 2001)

Obviously, the absolute retail sales figure used in this comparison does not depend only on the size of the country and its population but also on average *per capita* spending on organic food (Figure 2.6). Danish consumers spend more on organic food than consumers in any other country.

It is also interesting to compare a country's market share and estimated total retail sales of organic food and beverages with its percentage of organically cultivated land area (Figure 2.2). Production area does not always correlate with market share. For example, while Italy has by far the largest organically cultivated land area in Europe, it only ranks fourth in retail sales. Such discrepancies may be due to the fact that even within organic farming the intensity of land use varies widely. Large areas used for sheep production are typical in some Italian regions. Also of importance is the fact that Italy exports a large part of its organic products (Figure 2.7) and had only a small domestic market until 2000. *Per capita* spending on organic foods in Italy is far lower than in most other European countries, with Denmark, Switzerland and Sweden markedly higher (Figure 2.6).

Market segmentation

The organic farming sector has succeeded in establishing a market for its produce. This was only possible by segmenting the market into organic

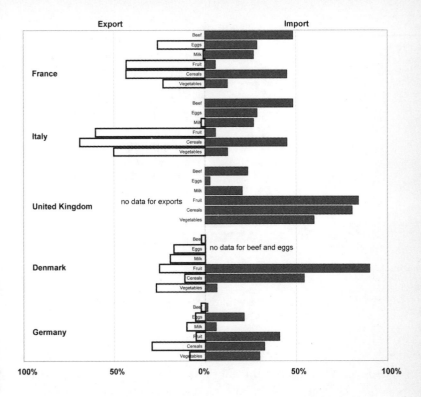

Figure 2.7 **Imports and exports of organic food products: shares by volume (%) of domestic markets for selected products and countries in 2000** (Hamm *et al.* 2002)

products and conventional products. This market segmentation paved the way for the growth of the organic farming sector over the last two decades. A necessary prerequisite for this market segmentation was a clearly defined production system guaranteed by control and certification systems. However, organic and conventional products are defined by the way in which the products are produced, not by the chemical, physical or biological properties of the product itself.

To establish a separate market for organic products, a number of consumers must perceive the quality of organic products to be higher than

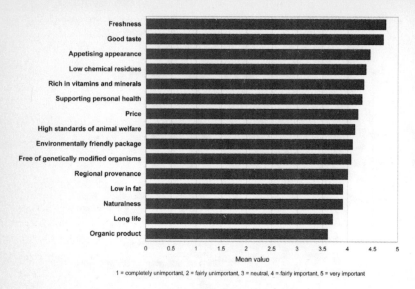

Figure 2.8   Criteria for the willingness to pay a price premium for food products (Müller and Hamm 2001)

the quality of conventional products. This can be a very subjective concept: quality is what consumers think it is. Quality can relate to the product's attributes, such as the perception that organic products are healthier, taste better, or are simply trendier or more fashionable. But quality can also relate to the consumer's wish to support a good cause – a better environment, less pollution or more regional production – which does not necessarily benefit them directly. Although many empirical studies show that these reasons play a role, albeit relatively small, in the demand for organic products, no uniform analyses of the whole European market based on an assessment of consumers' motives for purchasing organic products yet exist.[1]

The marketing of organic products needs to take consumers' motives for buying organic products into account. Consumers are not necessarily motivated by an adherence to organic principles; their choice in favour of organic products is more likely to reflect their general values, ethical standards, levels of personal satisfaction and well-being. For example, Müller and Hamm (2001) (Figure 2.8) showed that in Germany aspects such as taste or animal welfare are more important motives for buying food than organic principles, although animal welfare is stated as a principle in organic standards.

Surprisingly, the most important retailers' arguments for marketing organic food in Germany are quite different: environmental protection, food safety and health, taste and nature conservation (Michelsen *et al.* 1999).

In contrast, retailers in Italy appear to promote organic food with relevant arguments. Zanoli and Naspetti (2001) showed that the most important motives for buying organic products are linked to health and well-being; the most commonly used retailers' arguments in Italy are food safety, health and taste (Michelsen *et al.* 1999). A similar overlap between consumers' motives for buying organic food and retailers' sales arguments is observed in the UK (Makatouni 2001).

Overall, some value differences seem to exist among consumers in different parts of Europe. While animal welfare is a value almost unknown to Italian or Greek consumers, it plays an important role in the Northern European countries (Zanoli and Naspetti 2001). Similarly, environmental concerns and altruistic values seem to play a more important role in motivating Northern European consumers than Mediterranean ones. These results highlight the fact that consumer perception is not related directly to organic principles or to good taste or appetising appearance.

Consumers of organic food are mainly demotivated by high prices, poor product distribution, little obvious difference in quality, a lack of information on the nature of organic products, and doubts about their genuine organic origin (Schaer 2001; ZMP 2001; Zanoli and Naspetti 2001).

The perception of organic food and farming, and consequently the motivation/demotivation of consumers to buy organic food, can change quickly in response to such factors as marketing campaigns from the organic sector or food scares (Röder 2002).

Labelling

Even if consumers are willing to buy organic products and actively look for them in the market place, they must be able to recognise products as organic. In most European countries, some kind of label is used on organic products to signal that they are genuine. In some countries only one logo is used, while in others a range of logos, labels and brands exists. In Germany, for example, up to the year 2000 each of the nine existing producer associations used its own logo (Figure 2.9), although a national logo existed.

For the consumer, such a flood of information can be confusing (Zanoli *et al.* 2001b), with the result that consumers do not recognise any of the logos because none of them is sufficiently widely known. Confused consumers are also more likely to doubt that a product is genuinely organic,

Figure 2.9 The range of labels used by producer associations in Germany

especially as consumers seem to have more confidence in government-backed labels than in private brands (Roosen *et al*. 2001).

A positive example in this respect is Denmark, where a government label exists which is recognised by 100 per cent of all consumers and appears on 80 per cent of all organic products (Hamm *et al*. 2002). In contrast, the German national logo mentioned above had very little support in the marketplace (2 per cent) and was recognised by only 1 per cent of consumers (Hamm 2002). This logo was replaced by a well-supported government label in 2001.

Price premiums
Organic products are generally more expensive than conventional products (Figure 2.10). Some European consumers are willing to pay price premiums

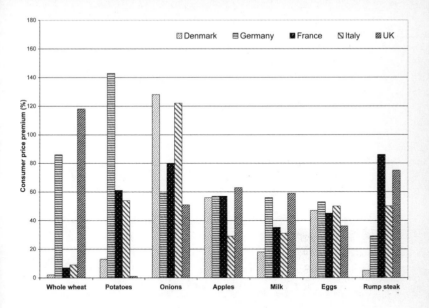

Figure 2.10 Price premiums paid by consumers for selected organic products in selected countries in 2000 (Hamm *et al.* 2002)

for organic products. However, consumers' willingness to buy organic food declines as price premiums increase. A 15–18 per cent price premium is considered adequate by most consumers (Schaer 2001). As a general rule, a 25–30 per cent price premium still seems to be acceptable to a broad range of consumers and thus to retailers attempting to reach broader segments of consumers. Much higher premiums seem to severely limit the number of potential purchasers. Interestingly, however, Marchesini (1992) showed that purchasing decisions are not always made on the basis of the actual market price but on the basis of what consumers believe to be the price at that moment. Owing to a lack of information, approximately 20 per cent of consumers do not detect price variations of up to 60 per cent. For these consumers, price is not an important factor in purchasing decisions.

Consumer price premiums tend to be high for countries and products with a small total turnover of organic production compared with conventional products. For example, high price premiums are achieved for vegetables, potatoes and fruit in several Mediterranean countries such as Italy, Spain, Greece and Portugal, despite their national production (Michelsen *et al.* 1999). By contrast, in countries where organic products

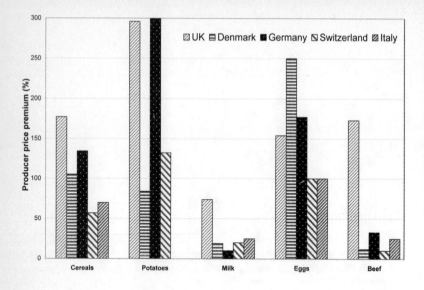

Figure 2.11 **Typical producer price premiums for selected organic products** (Hamm *et al.* 2002)

are sold in supermarkets, such as Austria, Denmark and Switzerland, lower premiums tend to be paid by the consumer (Michelsen *et al.* 1999).

The most obvious reason for price premiums for organic products is the lower yield level achieved in organic farming. Higher prices enable organic farmers to make profits per hectare similar to those realised by conventional farmers. However, the price premiums paid to producers do not always fully justify consumer price premiums (Figure 2.11), particularly for processed products where raw material is a small proportion of the total.

Processing and distribution

Another reason for price premiums for organic products is the efficiency of the transportation, processing and distribution system from the farm gate to the consumer. Although the organic food market has expanded impressively during the last decades in many European countries, its small size may in some ways be regarded as an obstacle to further growth. Economies of scale cannot come into effect for companies involved in the processing and distribution of organic food.

A small number of organic farmers spread over a wide area make it expensive and unattractive for processing firms and distributors to accept organic products. They would have to be processed separately in quantities too small for the system's design, especially when the major outlets for food, – supermarkets – are involved. Thus the small dimension of supply is a factor hampering market development (Michelsen et al. 1999). The potential consumer demand for organic products is therefore not necessarily matched with supply (Dienel 2000, Hamm and Michelsen 1996, Michelsen et al. 1999, Michelsen et al. 2001). This may also be the reason for the limited availability of organic products in supermarkets, which again makes it less attractive for consumers to buy organic products as they are used to a much broader range of products being offered in the conventional sector. In other words, if the consumers have to make additional efforts to buy organic products, by shopping in a variety of locations, they are less likely to buy them.

Increasing availability of supply and more efficient distribution of larger quantities are expected to help reduce price premiums to levels more acceptable to consumers. A closer look at the availability of organic products and the distribution structure of organic retail sales is therefore worthwhile.

Sales channels

The distribution structure of organic products seems to vary widely throughout Europe, as shown in Figure 2.12. For example, whereas in the Netherlands and Germany most sales still take place in specialist organic food shops, in most Scandinavian countries, the UK and Austria organic food is generally sold through supermarkets. In recent years, supermarkets and larger retail outlets have begun to stock a wider range of organic products and are becoming the main actors in the organic retail market, even in countries where historically a well-established and widespread network of specialised organic shops exists. This seems to promote the sales of organic food (Pinton et al. 2001) because new consumer segments are included, whereas specialised shops are mainly targeted at special groups of consumers looking for an alternative to mass-market outlets.

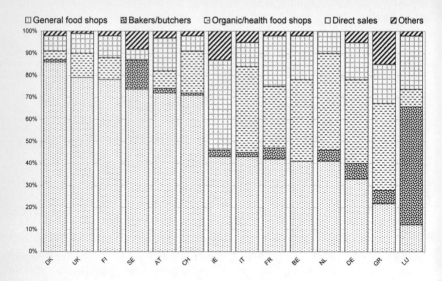

Figure 2.12 Distribution of sales channels for organic food in various European countries in 2000 (Hamm *et al.* 2002)

At the beginning of 2002 seven of the UK's top supermarket chains supported a campaign for a massive increase in organic farming (30 per cent of total agricultural land by 2010) and two out of three organic sales are made in the three largest multiple retailers in the UK (*World Organic News* 2002). As 70 per cent of food purchasing in the UK is done in supermarkets, such a campaign will have some effect on consumer awareness of organic products and demand, and thus impact back on production. Furthermore, supermarkets will be able to decrease the share of imported goods.

A glance at various strategies for organic markets in different countries provides a more comprehensive view of the reasons behind the variations in market share of organic products (Table 2.2). In countries where organic produce tends to be sold most successfully (Austria, Switzerland, Denmark and Sweden) and reaches a market share of more than 2 per cent, five aspects seem to coincide:

1 Strong consumer influence: consumers view organic products very positively and ask for them in the market.

2 Consumer price premium level: the price premium consumers have to pay when buying organic products instead of conventional products is smaller than 50 per cent.

3 Uniform labelling: a single marketing logo for products from different organic producer associations exists and is important.

4 Marketing through retail outlets: the market share of supermarkets and other conventional outlets – as opposed to health food shops and other specialised vehicles – is higher than 50 per cent.

5 Active promotion by large retailers: large retailing and processing firms actively promote organic products.

In sum, the organic food market in Europe seems to exhibit several characteristics which are typical for immature markets (Wier and Calverly 1999, cited in Michelsen *et al.* 1999):

1 Organic food is not labelled clearly.

2 In many countries, organic food has only recently become available in mainstream food retailers such as multiple retailers or supermarkets.

3 Distribution costs are high due to small quantities.

4 Consumer demand is not met by supply.

5 Marketing measures are undertaken by primary producers and processing/distribution companies tend to be amateurish.

If our readers are not yet convinced that imbalances still exist in the organic food market, it may be useful to look at relative price premiums in different countries. As indicated in figures 2.10 and 2.11, price premiums differ significantly between countries and, indeed, within countries. Economic theory suggests that this can be due to a poorly functioning market.

In a well-functioning market, demand and supply are balanced. Any changes in supply or demand are translated into a rise or a drop in market prices. As long as no trade tariffs exist, the price difference for a product in two countries should not be higher than the transportation cost. Within the EU, no trade tariffs or levies exist. Nevertheless, price premiums paid for organic products differ widely between countries. Evidence suggests that

Table 2.2   Marketing organic food in relation to its proportion of the total food market in various European countries in 1997/8 (Michelsen *et al*. 1999)

Market share of organic food in %[1]		Strong consumer influence	Consumer price premiums < 50%	Uniform labelling	Marketing through retail outlets > 50%	Active promotion by large retailers
> 2%	Switzerland	+	+	+	+	+
	Austria	+	+	+	+	+
	Denmark	+	+	+	+	+
	Sweden	+	−	+	+	+
1.1– 2.0%	Germany	+	−	−	−	+
	Luxembourg	−	−	−	−	−
	Finland	−	−	−	+	+
0.5– 1.0%	UK	+	+	−	+	+
	Italy [2]	−*	−	−	−	+
	Norway[2]	+	−	+	+	+
	Netherlands[2]	−	+	+	−	−
	Belgium[2]	−	+	+	−	−
	France	−	nd	+	−	+

[1] Average of the five most important product categories (vegetables, cereals, milk, potatoes, fruit)
[2] Estimates of organic products' share of the overall market for foodstuffs
+ Yes; − No
* Evaluation based on unpublished data by Zanoli *et al*. (2001a)
nd no data

this is partly due to a lack of transparency and information within the organic food market.

Institutions

A valuable perspective on organic farming arises if it is viewed not merely as a production system covering a certain market segment but also as a social movement (Michelsen *et al.* 2001). The organic farming movement is based on open criticism of mainstream agricultural practices, such as the use of external inputs, and the conscious decision to make only selective use of certain inputs. Organic farming, therefore, has developed largely outside the agricultural establishment and its institutions. Indeed, it was initiated by individuals and organisations which are not part of mainstream agriculture. The institutional arrangements of these organisations have clearly influenced the development of organic farming.

The independent development of organic farming typically passes through the following stages:

1 *Opposition*: the organic farming sector is established with a specific identity by a diverse coalition of farmers and non-farmers.

2 *Recognition*: organic farming gains political recognition through officially classified production standards.

3 *Support*: this is followed by a second wave of political support in the form of financial subsidies for organic farming.

In many cases, in parallel to political intervention in the organic sector, the following developments have taken place:

- A cooperative relationship between organic farming and the conventional farming community has evolved.

- An organic food market has developed which goes beyond local and regional entities.

If organic farming is compared to other agricultural sectors on an equivalent economic scale, it becomes quite clear that the roots of organic farming as a social movement still have important implications today. Most organic farming institutions try to remain independent of centralised powers. For example, while some countries try to unite their organic farmers around a single logo, attempts to establish international logos and trademarks within organic farming have had little success, despite the economies of scale expected in these projects.

Accordingly, political lobbying and representation of organic farming are very weak. In several European capitals, there is not a single full-time lobbyist promoting organic farming. Similarly, at the EU Commission's headquarters in Brussels, no powerful lobbying organisation exists which could provide the European Commission with ideas and information in support of organic farming.

The organic farming lobby in Europe lacks what most international enterprises take for granted:

- a centralised lobby;

- common presentation in the market place;

- professional and uniform public relations and marketing;

- good contacts with policy makers, consumer organisations and the media.

It is likely that the effective presence of professional lobbyists would have secured a more helpful and productive European regime for organic plant production in the years after 1991. A good example of what can be achieved by an effective lobby is offered by the European sugar lobby. A closely knit system of sugar lobbyists maintains good contacts with all important institutions and business partners within the agricultural sector. As a result, the sugar lobby has managed to keep the industry out of all reforms to the Common Agricultural Policy and to maintain high prices.

Although organic farming has won the sympathy of a considerable part of the European population, and is also in line with the current intentions of EU policy makers, its underdeveloped lobby means that it is not punching its political weight in comparison with other, better organised agricultural sectors.

Research and innovation

Priorities

Until the 1970s, organic food production had been developed mainly by experienced practitioners. The idealism of the organic farming movement and the researchers working in this area ensured that interest centred not only on production technology and methods but also on related philosophical and social issues.

The organised involvement of research institutions started in the 1970s; universities became involved in the mid-1980s and government institutions in the 1990s. As the interest of (mainly private) research institutions in organic farming increased, the traditional practitioners' trial-and-error approach was replaced by analytical research methodology (Niggli 1999).

In the past, research often focused on describing and analysing the organic farming system. This was most commonly based on comparative studies (Raupp 1994). Consequently, a range of interesting comparative research findings exist in this area. As well as problem-solving potential, these results offer a socio-political justification of organic farming.

Today, research in organic farming in most countries is intended to improve farm production techniques (Wynen and Vanzetti 1999). A trend towards process issues – food quality, environmental and social consequences, policy development, marketing – and a shift away from technical issues can be observed.

Several studies have looked in more detail at the most frequent priorities in research into organic farming (Figure 2.13) (Folli and Nasolini 1995;

EFRC 1996; Höök 1996; Wynen and Vanzetti 1999; Zerger 1999; Keatinge *et al.* 2000; Kolbe and Rikabi 2000). For example, the research priorities of all national, regional and private research institutes involved in organic farming research in Germany in 1998 centred on issues such as plant production (27 per cent), animal husbandry (12 per cent), agricultural economics (11 per cent), agricultural engineering (10 per cent), and horticulture and fruit production (17 per cent) (Kolbe and Rikabi 2000). On a European level, research programmes tend to include a very high proportion of studies on crop production, although there is an increasing shift towards livestock research. In countries such as the UK or Denmark, where livestock farming is important, a high overall proportion of livestock research is observed. In the Mediterranean region, research on horticulture predominates; here, research tends to have a regional character due to the great variations in climate, farming and cropping patterns.

In the above-mentioned example from Germany (Kolbe and Rikabi 2000), 63 per cent of researchers considered their research to be applied, while 30 per cent conducted applied as well as strategic and fundamental

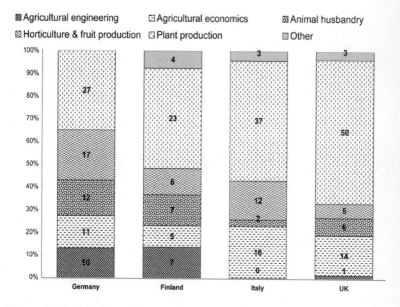

Figure 2.13 Priorities of research projects on organic farming: examples from various European countries

(Folli and Nasolini 1995; EFRC 1996; Höök 1996; Kolbe and Rikabi 2000)

research. Wynen and Vanzetti (1999) even conclude that hardly any basic research is undertaken on organic farming. Nevertheless, an evaluation of government-funded research by organic farming advisers (Zerger 1999) showed that a mere 20 per cent were satisfied with the degree to which research met the needs of farming practice. In comparison, more than 60 per cent did not see any satisfaction of the needs of farming practice, at least in most areas. Instead, the most urgent research priorities voiced by advisers related to specific practical problems, such as combating root weeds or potato blight. This discrepancy in perception seems to be due primarily to a lack of contact with farming practice in the planning and implementation of research, poor communication with the advisory system, and insufficient consideration of the systemic character of farms. The research results which had been successfully translated into practice had been initiated by practitioners. Findings are often not put into practice because they are presented poorly or are irrelevant to the practical work of organic farming (Zerger 1999). Although these results refer primarily to the interface between research and farming practice in general, they highlight the need for stakeholder involvement in setting research priorities.

From a more general point of view, research in organic farming aims to understand and improve the organic farming system as a whole. This includes the sector's medium- to long-term ecological stability and social/economic sustainability (Lindenthal et al. 1996). It should thus be possible to work out solutions for practical problems. This is determined by several interlinked factors: the productive capacity of the farming system; the skills and knowledge of the people involved; and markets, infrastructure and government policy.

Research work on organic farming in the EU can be categorised broadly as: long-term studies of farming systems (strategic), applied short-term projects (applied), and application of the results of research on conventional farming (applied/development) (Lampkin et al. 1999a). Research to support policy making is also part of the European research landscape. None of these research categories can be neglected.

In Europe, the countries with the highest shares of organic farming do not necessarily have the highest budgets for organic research, but funding seems to increase with the demand for organic products, growing public awareness and political pressure (Lampkin et al. 1999a). However, spending on research for organic farming still does not match the significance of organic farming. For example, under the EU research funding programmes of the late 1990s, the EU AIR and EU FAIR programmes, only about 3 per cent and 0.4 per cent of total funds was spent on pure organic farming projects (Lampkin *et al.* 1999a). Apart from the involvement of the EU in funding organic farming research in several countries, governmental bodies and private foundations have also made contributions towards research in organic farming. Nonetheless, the organic sector has developed largely outside the domain of the traditional research system (Lampkin *et al.* 1999a).

In general, research benefiting the general public directly is considered worthy of government funding. Usually, such policy-driven research relates to public goods such as environmental safety, public health or the rural economy. On the other hand, research that mainly benefits particular industries or companies tends to be funded by them. Examples of industry-driven research or research benefiting the general public include the design and testing of new consumer products or machinery.

As we have seen, specific organic farming research has been undertaken since organic farming came into existence. There is no doubt that research is vital for the future development of the agricultural sector. But are research and innovation specific to organic farming really necessary, or can general agricultural research develop organic farming without specifically targeting this system?

Specific organic farming research

Organic farming is a system that relies on the dynamic functional interaction between soil, plants, animals, humans, the ecosystem and the environment (IFOAM 1996) instead of external inputs such as pesticides or mineral fertiliser. This farming method views the farm as an organism which relies on varied crop-farming practices. It aims to protect the environment, restore and maintain soil fertility and produce high-quality agricultural products which contain no chemical residues (Box 1.1 and Box 1.2). This does not mean – as often argued by critics of organic farming (for example, Kirchmann and Thorvaldsson 2000) – that organic food production is a system preferred by romantics clinging to a nineteenth-century approach to agriculture without seeing that the world has changed (Dabbert 2000). On the contrary, organic farming is based on the conscious decision to make only selective use of modern technologies.

In principle, organic and conventional farmers face similar problems, and the general objective of research will always be to improve their respective farming systems. However, the remedies selected to address the problems encountered in these farming systems vary. Two separate aspects must therefore be considered. On the one hand, many innovations from conventional agricultural research have contributed – and can still contribute – to improving the organic farming system. For example, many advances in agricultural machinery or animal housing systems can be useful in organic as well as in conventional farming. On the other hand, many areas exist that are specific to organic farming and need to be addressed in this context. One example is plant pathology. As synthetic pesticides are not permitted for pest control, other measures must be exploited or developed. Another example is optimising nutrient cycles (primarily nitrogen). The ban on mineral nitrogen fertiliser in organic farming makes optimum nutrient management essential.

Some of these issues – which are vital for the success of organic farming – have been overlooked by conventional agricultural research. However, the majority of findings of research in organic farming have flowed back into conventional farming, such as the use of beneficial insects for pest control in greenhouse conditions.

Concern with the environment and food quality may be other areas in which knowledge and awareness gained from organic farming may benefit the development of conventional agriculture. Although these issues are not specific to the organic farming system itself, the movement has tried for a long time to find ways to address them, and the knowledge acquired can be put at the disposal of the whole agricultural sector.

In summary, the two most important reasons to pursue research specific to organic farming are:

- Different research problems exist in organic as compared to conventional farming.

- The stimulation of diversity in research can create synergies: issues ignored in conventional agriculture are dealt with in organic farming research. These results can be put to work in agriculture in general.

Research methodologies
Ever since the traditional practitioners' trial-and-error approach in organic farming was replaced by analytical research methodologies in the 1980s and 1990s, a more holistic approach to research has been demanded by the organic farming movement. However, according to Niggli (1998), a consensus on what constitutes holism has not been reached. While some people define holistic research as the study of crop and pasture carried out in line with the concept of crop rotations, others consider on-farm research

with farmer involvement to be holistic. Another approach to holistic research is to use inter/multidisciplinary approaches, integrating socio-economic and agronomic research as in Raupp's assessment (1994: 84): 'It obviously must include the people in agriculture; without question they should have socially just and ethically defensible living and working conditions.' Perhaps the system concept best describes the term holistic; this is based on the view that the interaction of the whole system is more than the sum of its parts (Dewes 1994).

Little progress has been made in finding ways to implement the holistic concept in practice (Niggli and Lockeretz 1996). An example from the German-speaking countries (Germany, Austria, Switzerland)[2] presented in Figure 2.14 reflects this. In reality, most research efforts are still undertaken on a disciplinary basis by one research organisation, and disciplinary research based on traditional research approaches seems to prevail (Gerber 2001).

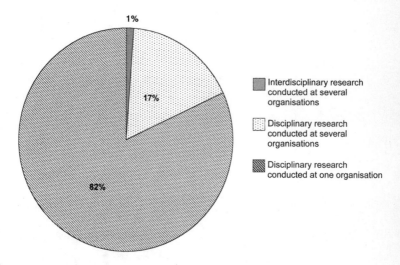

Figure 2.14 Organisational approach to organic farming research
(Gerber 2001)

In contrast, Table 2.3 presents an appraisal of the differences between conventional and organic research as assessed by a work group of experts. This not only provides a good picture of the lack of consensus on the nature of organic research within the group; it also provides a strict demarcation of organic *vis-à-vis* conventional farming research.

Table 2.3   **The differences between conventional and organic research as assessed by a work group of experts**
(Keatinge and Rasmussen 1999)

Organic	Conventional
Multi/interdisciplinary	Discipline-based
Interdependence of activities	Singularity of activities
Role of value judgement/intuition	Objectivity
Longer-term	Short-term
Environmental interaction	Environmental control
Greater range of parameter studies	Fewer parameters evaluated
Based on farmers' goals	Involves 'commercial' goals
Applied	Fundamental

Considering the trend towards multi/interdisciplinary approaches in all agricultural research today, this clear distinction between research of organic and conventional farming systems seems no longer appropriate.

However, Table 2.3 does illustrate the need to take full account of the inherent complexity of the system, rather than seeking to reduce or avoid complexity altogether, when investigating organic farming. The challenge is to develop approaches that embrace as many of these interactions as possible.

This implies that

- no relation with the system may be disregarded, including future ones;

- research must take multiple points of view, from within (researchers as subjective 'actors') and from the outside (researchers as objective observers); and that

- a holistic approach to research may be applied to different degrees but a high level of interdisciplinarity and integration always exists, and attention to farmers and their values is often considered important (Alrøe et al. 1998).

Systematic gathering and analysis of information can provide an overall picture of the broader context (Hansen and Ruissen 1999). In accordance with good scientific practice, research in organic farming must be problem-oriented and appropriate methods must be selected. Researchers should not hesitate to use traditional methods if they are best suited to a specific problem. However, this does not imply that methods developed to suit the specific problems of research on organic food and farming do not comply with good scientific practice. A criticism sometimes voiced by opponents of organic farming is that organic farming standards and, therefore, research into organic farming, do not have a sound scientific basis.

Scientific research is never value-free and values determine the research questions asked. The organic farming movement has chosen a set of values stated in their production standards (IFOAM 1996). Instead of differentiating the organic research approach from the conventional one, it can be considered compliant to systems theory, as is widely acknowledged.

Organisation

The organisation of research for organic farming began in the 1970s. This led to the establishment of two types of private research institute, differentiated by their interest in either

- organic gardening or small-scale farming; or

- professional, full-time organic farming.

A good example of the first type of research organisation is the Henry Doubleday Research Association (HDRA) in the UK (Box 2.1, p. 38). The second type is well represented by the Elm Farm Research Centre (UK) (Box 2.2), the Research Institute of Organic Agriculture (Forschungs-institut für biologischen Landbau – FiBL) in Switzerland, and the Ludwig Boltzmann Institute for Organic Agriculture and Applied Ecology (near Vienna, Austria).

In the 1980s, the universities began to appoint the first professors in organic farming, among them H. Vogtmann in Witzenhausen, Germany. By the 1990s, most European countries were approving state-funded research programmes and organic research centres. Examples are the Danish Research Centre (DARCOF) at Foulum, the Finnish Research Station for Ecological Agriculture at Juva, and the German Institute of Organic Farming of the Federal Research Agency (Bundesforschungsanstalt für Landwirtschaft – FAL) at Trenthorst.

Among these institutions, three different organisational models seem to prevail:

- private foundations with strong links to the organic movement and an increasing level of state-funded activities (FiBL, for example);

Box 2.1   Self-portrait: the Henry Doubleday Research Association (HDRA 2001)

HDRA is Europe's largest organic association. It is dedicated to research-ing and promoting organic gardening, farming and food.

- HDRA's International Research Department is working to improve commercial organic farming/cultivation in Britain.

- Its Information and Education Department provides advice to over 28,000 members and regularly advises the media, industry and statutory bodies. HDRA staff write books and articles for the national press, and appear regularly on television and radio.

- The organisation runs a consultancy service on organic garden design and landscaping, large-scale composting and waste management, and organic product retailing.

- HDRA's three organic display gardens at Ryton near Coventry, Yalding near Maidstone, and Audley End near Saffron Walden are open to the public and attract thousands of visitors each year. It also runs food, gardening and gift shops at its three sites, selling one of the best ranges of quality organic products in the UK, and has restaurants at Ryton and Yalding.

- HDRA's Heritage Seed Library saves hundreds of old and unusual vegetable varieties for posterity, also distributing them to its members. Anyone can join.

- HDRA's Overseas Programme carries out research and advisory work with organisations throughout the tropics to develop and promote organic practices of benefit to small-scale farmers. HDRA's Third World Organic Support Group helps to fund this work.

- HDRA works with Chase Organics Ltd. to produce *The Organic Gardening Catalogue*, offering, by mail order, the very best selection of organic products in the country. HDRA also runs The Organic Wine Club in association with Vinceremos Wines.

- HDRA holds National Potato Days, National Organic Gardening Week-ends and dozens of other events.

- At the time of writing, HDRA, with its associated trading company Organic Enterprises Ltd., has 125 members of staff, who continually strive to promote excellence in all things organic.

Box 2.2   **Self-portrait: Elm Farm Research Centre** (EFRC 2001)

Elm Farm Research Centre was founded in 1980 as an educational charity. Our aim is the development and promotion of organic agriculture as the most environmentally sound way of producing healthy food.

As an educational charity, it is important for EFRC to get its information, knowledge and experience out into the public domain. This is achieved not only through the Organic Advisory Service and Education Services but also through written material — articles, scientific papers, contributions to books and our own *Bulletin*. Internationally, we collaborate with IFOAM, universities and research bodies, farmers' groups and individuals.

EFRC is based on a 237-acre (96-ha), fully converted working farm in Berkshire. The farm provides a base for EFRC's research and educational work as well as being a commercial farming and marketing operation. It is also a facility for community activities; the farm is the basis for a new approach to local economic development. The EFRC library houses a collection of reference works on organic agriculture in the UK. It is available to anyone who wants to see it. Elm Farm is the home of four independent small businesses — Organic Resource Agency, a share-farming sheep operation, Period Plants and a traditional underwoodsman — all of which are building ecologically sound, locally based enterprises.

- research centres resulting from a public effort to coordinate public and private research in organic farming, following a strategy agreed among research institutions and organic stakeholders on a nationwide basis: DARCOF, a research centre 'without walls', is an example (Box 2.4);

- research centres representing the idea that organic farming is another product of agricultural research – like soil science or horticulture – that needs to be tackled in a separate, state-funded research centre such as the recently established Institute for Organic Farming at FAL.

Previous sections have formulated the following demands: (1) the need for specific organic research; (2) the striving for a maximum integration of all aspects of the organic farming system and the development of a more holistic research approach; and (3) the need to bring all stakeholders together in order to set priorities. We can now summarise important organisational aspects of research in organic farming that can meet these demands.

Box 2.3   Portrait of the Research Institute of Organic Agriculture (FiBL) (FiBL 2003)

The Research Institute of Organic Agriculture is active in almost every area of organic farming, although recently FiBL has chosen to concentrate on research, advisory services and training and education.

- It has four research divisions: soil and plant production; livestock; landscape and economics; advice and training.
- Extension directly related to research is a core competence and strength of FiBL. Many projects are on-farm projects directly linked to the farmers' needs, thus showing that demand is the driving factor, with much cross-fertilisation and innovation.
- Good connections to stakeholders is another strength. The holistic research approach and its focus on ethical questions in organic farming make FiBL an interesting benchmark for many other institutes in and outside Switzerland.
- Research cooperation with the Swiss Federal Research Institute funded by the Swiss Federal Office of Agriculture: its Therwil trial has a worldwide reputation.
- In 1993 BIO SUISSE and FiBL were awarded accreditation by the Swiss Federal Government to act as inspection and certification bodies for organic farming in accordance with Standard EN 45011. However, in 1999 inspection services were divested to the public limited company BIO.INSPECTA AG.

If we conclude that specific organic farming research is needed, there are also good arguments for organising this separately, if not in isolation, from conventional farming research. It is not only that the priorities tend to be different from research priorities in conventional farming; researchers not familiar with organic agriculture are also unable to judge research priorities adequately, or to decide on an appropriate distribution of funds.

A maximum integration of all aspects of the organic farming system is best achieved by multi/interdisciplinary research teams. The desired integration into a functional whole needs to be kept in mind from the beginning to the end of the research process.

In general, agricultural research organisations must offer various services apart from the pure research services (client-oriented innovation development and the generation of decision-enabling information): technology transfer services, scientific services and technical services. To facilitate

---

Box 2.4   Self-portrait: Danish Research Centre for Organic Farming (DARCOF 2001)

DARCOF was set up in 1996 with the aim of maximising the returns from resources allocated for research. In contrast to the situation in many other countries, no Danish institutes specialise exclusively in research in organic farming. The remit of DARCOF was, and is, to initiate and co-ordinate a concerted research effort in organic farming. The research must contribute to the development of organic farming and the sustainable development of agriculture. DARCOF should also contribute to the education of researchers, agricultural advisers and teachers, and communicate the results of the research.

Research at many different levels in the agricultural system can be of relevance to organic farming. DARCOF was established as a 'centre without walls' where the actual research is performed in interdisciplinary collaboration between the participating research groups, which are situated at various research institutions. By drawing on research groups in different disciplines, it is possible to use their knowledge and expertise in addressing the complex problems of organic farming. Synergistic interactions are encouraged through collaboration between different research environments and the complementary nature of research in organic farming and other disciplines.

---

these services in a client-oriented way – in the case of organic farmers, for example – close links between researchers and their clients must be maintained.

Core centres of competence with core funds for a permanent infrastructure are needed to facilitate integration of direct research and accompanying services, at the regional as well as the national and international level (Häring and Dabbert 2002). A leading institution, a permanent forum of researchers or simply a facilitating coordinating body could provide such a permanent infrastructure. However, permanent public funding is crucial for their maintenance. Who will provide this funding? Funding from private enterprise is not likely: the organic farming segment is too small and does not need mineral fertiliser or pesticides. Thus, public funding is crucial for centres of competence to provide their services.

Concerted action is necessary for a sustainable development of the organic farming sector. Research can play an important part in this development because it can provide the necessary information.

Therefore, funding corresponding to the current and potential significance of organic farming is required for the sound development of the sector. If target values have already been set (in 2001, for example, Germany set the goal of a 20 per cent share for organic farming by 2010), research has to be expanded significantly beforehand in order to assist the development by generating the needed information and providing advice. However, information required today is not usually supplied tomorrow; neither do adequately educated researchers evolve overnight.

European policies for organic farming in the 1990s

In the EU, two major and a number of minor political initiatives have been concerned with organic farming. This section gives an overview of the policies that were important in the European Union up to the end of the twentieth century.

The two most important EU policy measures, in terms of their impact on the organic farming sector, were

• the agri-environmental policies implemented as a consequence of the McSharry Reform (1992) of European agriculture policies, within which organic farming was supported;

• a Europe-wide common certification system for organic farming which came into effect at the beginning of the 1990s and has recently been extended to the animal production sector.

Further information on a number of other measures of minor importance for the general development of the organic farming sector can be found elsewhere (Lampkin et al. 1999a and b).

In financial terms, the agri-environmental support programmes (Council Regulation 2078/92) (EC 1992) are the most important European policy applicable to organic farming. Lampkin et al. (1999a) report that of a total of about €300 million spent on organic farming support in the EU (estimate for 1996), nearly €190 million was spent on these programmes. In the following year, this actually increased to €260 million. All other areas are – in financial terms – much less important.

Agri-environmental support
The reform of the Common Agricultural Policy in 1992 has been the most important change in direction of European agricultural policy in recent

decades. Named the McSharry Reform after the Agriculture Commissioner who was responsible at the time, it consisted of mainstream measures and others officially called the accompanying measures. This nicely describes the budget these measures received in relation to the mainstream measures. Yet these accompanying measures were quite important for organic farming. They were intended to provide a framework allowing environmentally friendly farming practices to be supported through specific regional or member state programmes. The measures included:

- Substantial reductions in the use of fertilisers and plant protection products.
- A reduction of the density of sheep and cattle per forage area.
- Long-term set-aside schemes.
- Support for organic farming – quite important in our context.

It was also possible to provide some support for demonstration and training projects on environmentally sustainable agriculture.

In line with the principle of subsidiarity, it was up to the member states and regions to devise and implement specific programmes, although these were subject to the approval of the European Commission. The regions had to finance 10–50 per cent of the expenditure in these programmes, while the rest was financed by the European Commission (50–75 per cent) and member states.

When it came to devising attractive agri-environmental programmes, responses from the regions/countries were quite diverse. In some countries, these programmes became a cornerstone of agricultural policy. In Austria in 1997, for example, agri-environmental support was claimed on more than 90 per cent of total agricultural land area (see first column, Table 2.4). In other countries – Greece, for example – participation in the programmes offered was close to zero because they were not very attractive.

The basic approach of the agri-environmental programmes is that farmers enter a voluntary contract with a governmental agency. The farmers commit themselves to specific farming practices that are perceived to be beneficial to the environment and receive a certain amount of money in return. Contracts are usually made on a five-year basis. A control system inspects a small sample (usually 5 per cent) of the farmers to check whether they actually abide by their commitments.

With respect to organic farming in Europe, the details of the agri-environmental programmes are as diverse as the programmes themselves.

Table 2.4   Agri-environmental support and organic farming in 1997 (Lampkin *et al.* 1999a and b, Michelsen *et al.* 1999, Foster and Lampkin 1999)

Country	Share of land in agri-environmental programmes (%)	Share of organic farming in expenditure on agri-environmental programmes (%)	Organic land share (%)
Austria	93.8	12.9	10.1
Finland	92.8	7.6	4.7
Italy	10.3	25.6	4.3
Sweden	55.4	17.0	3.8
Denmark	3.9	58.2	2.4
Germany	31.8	6.0	2.3
Netherlands	1.7	0.8	0.8
Ireland	21.2	nd	0.5
Luxembourg	74.3	nd	0.5
Belgium	1.4	23.7	0.5
Spain	2.8	3.9	0.6
France	22.7	1.4	0.6
Portugal	13.8	1.9	0.3
UK	8.9	0.9	0.7
Greece	0.7	31.7	0.3
EU 15	18.2	10.7	1.7

nd = no data

In France and in the UK, up to 2000 only the transition period was subsidised and after this no subsidies were paid. In all other countries, both organic farming in transition and continuing organic farming are supported by payments in the agri-environmental programmes. However, the size of the payment may or may not differ between the transitional and the continuing organic period. Some countries differentiate payments by crop type while others do not. In that case, area payments are usually higher for vegetable production, intensive horticulture, fruit, olives and wine production, while less is paid for cereal and grass forage. An example of the diversity of subsidies paid is given for cereals in fully converted organic production in Figure 2.15.

For example, an Austrian organic farmer received €326 per hectare for cereal in 1997, while UK farmers did not receive anything. Obviously, such differences have severe implications for fair competition. To tilt the playing

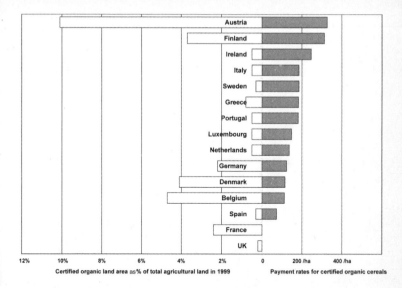

Figure 2.15 Typical payment rates for certified organic cereal in 1997
(Lampkin *et al.* 1999a and b; Foster and Lampkin 1999)

field even further in their favour, Austrian farmers could usually count on receiving an additional €50 of basic environmental support.

In most countries, the organic land supported by the agri-environmental programmes is a substantial proportion of the total certified organic area, which already points to the importance of these programmes for the development of organic farming in Europe (Figure 2.16). One interesting case is Sweden, where the policy-supported organic land is larger than the certified area, reflecting a specific strategy with respect to organic farming.

This is a case in point that might be useful in demonstrating that countries have different intentions in shaping their support programmes for organic farming, and that the role of these subsidies is interpreted very differently in different countries and different situations.

If organic farming is solely supported because of its environmental advantages, and at the same time the market is regarded as too small to take up further organic products without eroding the price premiums paid for organic products, it makes sense to support organic farming even though part of its output is marketed as conventional produce.

On the other hand, if the market demand is growing and there is perceived to be an opportunity to overcome bottlenecks within the food

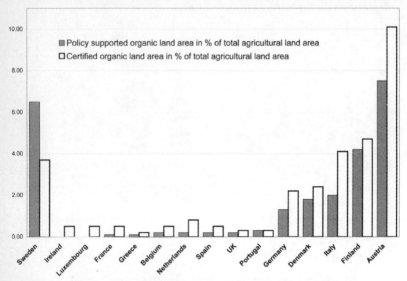

Figure 2.16 Policy-supported and certified organic land as a percentage of total agricultural land in 1997
(Foster and Lampkin 2000)

processing and distribution chain by increasing the quantities produced, it can make sense to support all certified and non-certified organic farming but encourage formal certification of all organic producers who want to receive subsidies. That way, all organic products are readily available to the organic market.

However, this support strategy needs to be treated with some caution. Assuming that (1) consumer demand for organic products does not increase, and (2) no major savings in the processing and distribution chain can be achieved by further growth, high enough subsidy payments to organic farmers will – so says economic theory – eventually lead to a complete erosion of price premiums, and separate organic markets will vanish.

Such erosion of price premiums due to financial support of organic farming is acceptable if organic farming is seen solely as a mechanism to provide public goods like environmental protection. But if market potential is to be developed, price premiums need careful monitoring (Michelsen *et al.* 1999) and demand-supporting measures should be encouraged.

In general, the second strategy – subsidies to increase supply – has been the more popular. The objective of this type of support is to increase the extent of organic farming. Obviously, farmers react to subsidies but, on the other hand, the decision of farmers to convert to organic farming depends on a number of factors, of which direct subsidisation of the production method is just one.

Farmers usually weigh up all their options before they convert to organic farming. The most important option is to continue to farm conventionally, maybe even under an agri-environmental programme other than organic farming. This programme might be financially attractive but with much less restriction on production technology than organic farming. In that case, farmers would most likely not choose organic farming.

Macroeconomic factors may also alter the effects of the introduction of direct subsidies for organic farming and the conversion process. One example is the United Kingdom, where the introduction of a subsidy in 1995 did not have much impact. In the existing macroeconomic climate, the subsidies were too low to be an incentive to convert. Only when depression hit the conventional farming economy did conversion take off.

Other important factors in the decision to convert are farmers' confidence in the reliability of a given subsidy and their assessment of future market development – especially of the price premiums they expect to receive for organic products.

All these factors taken together indicate that direct payments are not an automatic solution: a mere flick of the switch will not increase the extent of organic farming. However, empirical evidence suggests that a strong commitment by regional and country governments to supporting a large part of the organic area through agri-environmental programmes and to paying above-average subsidies generally contributes to a higher level of organic farming in those countries (Figure 2.16). In the case of increasing demand, subsidisation of supply can help to develop processing and marketing structures to levels where economies of scale can come into effect. Prices may erode quickly at constant demand.

Standards, Certification and Labelling

Organic farming could be considered as a production system in which farmers merely comply with certain standards. In this case, no certification system would be necessary. However, if products are to be marketed separately, a system ensuring that products have been produced according to organic standards must be established and a clear distinction between organic and conventional products needs to be pursued throughout the organic distribution and processing chain. The main objective of such a certification system is to assure consumers that products genuinely have been produced organically. As there is no obvious way for consumers to distinguish whether a product is organic, a price premium for organic products can only be achieved if confidence in the organic quality is ensured. This makes clear standards, certification and labelling of products important factors for the economic success of organic farming.

An outside observer might thus expect to find a clear and comprehensible system of standards, certification and labelling anywhere in the world. Yet the current situation in the EU is quite different. Council regulations 2092/91 and 1804/1999 (EC 1999a) define the standards to which farmers have to adhere in order to produce organically. While sometimes complicated in detail, these standards provide a clear basis for all organic farmers in Europe. Anyone who wants to sell products as organic can only do so by sticking to the rules laid out in the European regulations and submitting to an elaborate inspection system that has been set up to make sure that the products have been produced according to the standards. These standards also apply to those who want to export products into the European Union.

In order to understand this system better, it is useful to distinguish between *standards*, *certification*, and *labelling*.

Standards

The standards set by the EU can be seen as a minimum level within the Union. These standards explicitly state that stricter rules may be used. A number of stricter standards set out by national farmers' organisations – also belonging to the organic farming sector – exist. They can be interpreted in a number of different ways.

On the one hand, they can reflect regional differences in production conditions or even in consumer expectations, as most of these farmers' associations operate only on a regional or country level. On the other hand, stricter standards can be considered as a means to gather the 'true believers' in the idea of organic farming around the flag of these stricter standards, more closely reflecting the original ideas of organic farming. From a marketing point of view, stricter standards can be seen as the basis for further market segmentation within organic farming in an attempt to receive an additional premium for being the 'most organic' among the organic farmers.

Prior to European regulation of organic farming, most national standards were set by private sector bodies. The common standard introduced by regulation has had a major positive impact on both market transparency and trade opportunities, and clearly counteracts any attempt at fraud.

Yet it needs to be recognised that, with regulation, the basic power to define organic farming has shifted to government authorities. In some cases, these are detached from the organic sector and in many cases they are not 'true believers' in the organic system. Furthermore, organic farming thus becomes part of a legislative process that in Western democracies is heavily influenced by competing interest groups, both within and outside the organic farming sector.

The difficulty in securing common European regulation of animal production is an example of influence from within the sector. Let's take the example of standards for keeping organic dairy cows. Varying structural and natural conditions within the EU have led to methods of rearing dairy cattle that differ substantially across countries and regions. Where fields belonging to a single farm are small and scattered across a vast area, it might be quite difficult or even impossible to guarantee – at feasible cost – that dairy cows enjoy access to pasture throughout the summer. Organic farmers from regions with such structural conditions tend to be in favour of loosely formulated versions of standards regarding the requirements for pasture. In contrast, organic dairy farmers from regions with more favourable structural conditions may perceive this as an opportunity to get rid of competitors from those regions by setting stricter standards.

Although the organic farming sector is still quite small, its very existence is a challenge to industries supplying the inputs to agriculture which organic farming does not use. Such industries might have an interest in lobbying against any regulation of organic farming. However, it is not altogether clear whether such a lobbying strategy would be more successful if it advocated stricter standards – in the hope that few could meet them, keeping the sector small – or supported more loosely defined standards: allowing the use of GMOs, say, with the intention of making organic farming indistinguishable from integrated practices. Whatever the outcome, it has to be recognised that organic farming changes its character when its defining authority comes to be more closely identified with government.

Certification

Standards only become effective with the introduction of a system that guarantees adherence. The European certification system, based on the regulations for organic farming, was established for this purpose. Organisations that use stricter standards set up their own certification systems

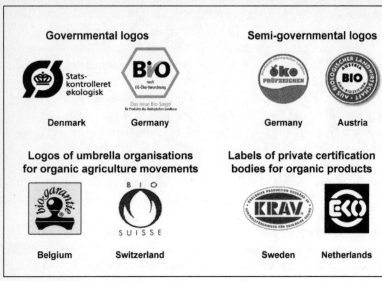

Figure 2.17 Different types of logos for organic products in Europe

guaranteeing those aspects of their standards that go beyond European rules. In practice, both types of certification can often be combined and just one control visit to the farm or the processer is necessary. The administration of the certification systems varies widely in different countries (see Lampkin *et al.* 1999b), although the European Commission supervises its effective functioning.

Labelling

Logos, labels and brands help the consumer to recognise organic products. For a long time this has been of concern only to some national governments and not to European policy. In December 1999, however, a European logo was introduced to communicate the organic character of a product clearly to consumers. Unfortunately, so far this logo has failed to find wide acceptance in the marketplace. Instead, a multitude of different logos and labels are used throughout Europe (Figure 2.17). Most of these are supported by farmers' organisations; others are government-supported. Typically these logos and labels designate specifics of the country of origin. A few exceptions which try to stress the international transferability of organic products exist, such as the Demeter logo indicating biodynamic production. The existence of too many logos is not only confusing for consumers, but tends

Figure 2.18 EU logos for designated origin compared to the organic farming logo

to produce an 'information entropy' effect (Zanoli *et al.* 2001b): consumers do not recognise any logo, because no one logo is sufficiently widely known.

A number of supermarket chains have started specific brands for organic products which are sold only in their supermarkets. In this area, national approaches also predominate. The difference between brands on the one hand and logos and labels on the other is quite important. A brand name is a 'private product' for which cost and benefit are borne by the respective supermarket chain, whereas logos and labels have the character of 'club goods'. Everybody who joins the club by paying dues and abiding by the club's rules can enjoy the benefits. The bigger the club, the more difficult it becomes to coordinate the diverging interests regarding the logo or label. And as the club gets bigger, individual members become less likely to promote the good of the club good. The more members the club has, the smaller the exclusivity of its benefits.

Thus an organic farmer who wants to use the European logo (Figure 2.18) will only benefit from using it if it is already widely recognised by consumers. Promoting a logo or label to establish it in the market and achieve its wide recognition demands collective action by the 'owners' of the logo. This is very expensive and demands a long-term approach.

The European logo for organic farming has two major advantages:

1 It is free of charge. Anybody who produces certified organic products may use it at no additional cost.

2 It is applicable in all EU countries, thus facilitating trade.

On the other hand, the European logo also has severe drawbacks:

1 It is neither actively promoted nor supported by a marketing campaign.

2 It is very similar to other European logos under the 'designated origin' legislation (Council regulations 2081/92 and 2082/92) (Figure 2.18).

3 It cannot be used for organic products with more than 5 per cent imported (to the EU) ingredients. This is a major obstacle to the use of the logo in many cases.

The widespread adoption of the European organic logo and its acceptance among consumers would most likely have positive effects on market transparency and consumer demand for organic products. For several reasons, however, there is room for different labels within Europe:

• Different labels often refer to different standards and the consequent market differentiation within organic farming.

• A multitude of labels and logos, as opposed to a single European logo that totally dominates the organic market, acts as a safety net for producers when food scares occur. Although the certification system seems to be quite effective, the possibility of scares still exists: if conventional food is being sold as organic, for example, or a contamination scare occurs in one country (as the Nitrofen scandal did in Germany in 2002). In such cases consumers tend to avoid any product associated with the logo concerned. A market segmentation that provides more than one logo in the market limits the effects of such scares. It can be indicated that only one of the organic market segments was involved.

The umbrella organisation of the organic agriculture movements, IFOAM (International Federation of Organic Agriculture Movements), is a non-profit organisation. IFOAM has developed an approach which in principle could be an alternative to government logos. The IFOAM seal indicates accreditation of national certification. However, it is not an approval or endorsement of the product itself. For certification bodies the seal means a strengthening of their certification symbol. For consumers, the IFOAM seal is intended to bring order in the chaos of logos. For producers, processers and packers it means better (equal) market access and a statement of dedication to integrity and private standards in addition to the various public regulations. For the organic movement as a whole it represents one global organic guarantee system (IOAS 1999). To indicate this accreditation the firm IOAS (International Organic Accreditation Service) has implemented an accreditation scheme and a seal (Box 2.5).

The IFOAM seal (Figure 2.19) is always used in conjunction with national certification logos. The strengths of this approach are as follows:

**Box 2.5   The International Organic Accreditation Service:
definition and statement of purpose** (IOAS 2001)

The IOAS is a non-profit, independent company registered and head-
quartered in the United States with satellite offices in Europe. It was
established by IFOAM in 1997 to run the IFOAM Accreditation Programme, which had been run by IFOAM itself since 1992. The IOAS
operates the Accreditation Programme under licence from IFOAM.

The sole purpose of the IOAS is to offer international oversight of
organic certification through an accreditation process for certification
bodies active in this field.

The standards and requirements against which applicants are judged
are the IFOAM Basic Standards and Criteria — requirements developed
by the international organic industry with organic integrity, transparency and stakeholder participation as core values.

The IFOAM Accreditation Programme is an industry-based global
guarantee of organic integrity, unburdened by national barriers and
implemented by one body which has no other interests.

Through a rigorous audit process that complies with international
accreditation norms, we help in building a common organic currency, so
that producers, processers and traders can go about their business con-
fidently and efficiently, and consumers can trust the label they read.

- It is a worldwide approach.

- It is dominated by IFOAM standards but not by
  any government, so there is no sign of industrialised countries dominating others.

- It acknowledges the diversity within the organic
  movement by adding the accreditation seal to
  different seals with different backgrounds.

**Figure 2.19   IFOAM
seal, which can be
used in conjunction
with national logos**

Among the weaknesses are:

- It is not in itself a guarantee of a product – but of certification; most consumers will be more interested in the product than in certification.

- There is insufficient money available to communicate this approach to
  the consumer; as a result, the IFOAM accredited seal is not well
  known.

- IFOAM itself is not as well known to consumers as other non-profit organisations like Greenpeace or the World Wildlife Fund (WWF). This limits its credibility.

While the IFOAM seal is gaining more support in the market, it is still not in a position to be a major player. A list of IFOAM-accredited certification bodies as of June 2001 indicated only 27 bodies worldwide. Why don't more certification bodies, and especially owners of labels, add the IFOAM seal to their labels and logos?

Obviously, many of them do not see any advantage in doing so because they are well known in their market segments. Nor would using the seal gain them new consumers, as consumers do not recognise the IFOAM seal. On the contrary, the use of the little-known IFOAM seal with a well-known logo benefits the IFOAM seal – a benefit that might then be captured by other suppliers with possibly even lower standards.

This argument indicates that within a large market like the EU it can make sense to link standards directly with a logo. In principle, this is the case with the EU organic logo. It also indicates that an umbrella logo is more likely to be accepted by existing market players if it can offer considerable benefits, including marketing efforts with financial backing and added credibility.

Thus the European policies tackling standards, certification and labelling have been quite successful in overcoming the major difficulties in developing standards and have established an efficient certification system. Although in both areas, private systems exist in addition to the European system, the European system has become the point of reference – even for those interested in stricter systems.

The third pillar of the policies dealing with organic farming – labelling – is intended to guarantee and communicate to the consumer the fact that organic farming is different from conventional farming. Until very recently this area of labels, logos and brands was dominated by private sector and national approaches.

Although the case for (limited) differentiation by various logos can be argued, there is a strong case for a widely used, politically backed European logo. A European logo exists already but its application is not yet widespread. Better adoption of this logo would require a major and long-term marketing campaign by the logo's owner, the European Union – and before such a campaign is launched, the concept of the current logo should be carefully assessed from a practical marketing perspective.

The development of organic farming in selected countries

The European organic farming sector and the main factors influencing the development of organic farming in Europe have been described briefly in earlier sections. Very different stages of development are observed in different European countries (Figure 2.20) and, even within countries, organic farming distribution is regionalised.

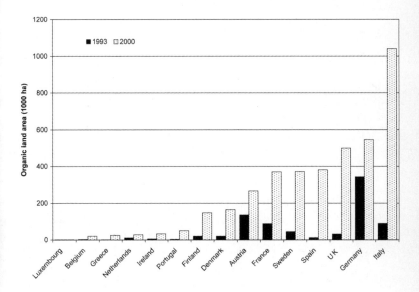

Figure 2.20 The development of organic land area and farms in Europe (based on Lampkin 2001)

Equally, markets for organic products expose strong national differentiation, not only with respect to market size and dynamics, price premiums, processing, distribution and sales channels, and import/export volumes, but also in terms of consumer motivation, sales arguments and labelling. A combination of these characteristics seems to have determined the development of the organic farming sector. The institutional settings and the different official policy environments have also contributed to the diverse development observed within the EU. An arbitrary combination of factors and influences ensures that no two countries are alike in that respect.

Four country case studies are described in more detail below to highlight the interaction of the different factors described in previous sections and the effect they had on the development of the organic farming sector in that country. These case studies are based on information from Lampkin (2001), Compagnoni et al. (2001), Fibiger Nørfeldt (2001), Foster and Lampkin (1999), Källander (2001), Lampkin et al. (1999), Michelsen et al. (2001), Nieberg et al. (2001), and Padel and Michelsen (2001).

Denmark was chosen because it is the most frequently mentioned example of a country with a well-developed organic farming sector which is based on a series of political commitments in the past. Sweden is presented due to its specific feature of supporting organic farming without demanding certification, which has led to a large organic farming area as well. Italy is presented because it has recently experienced a boom in organic farming. Finally, the UK is presented as an example of a country where organic farming, despite a long tradition, only recently experienced considerable growth rates after a period of stagnation.

Denmark

In 1987, Denmark was the first European country to introduce national organic standards and subsidies for the conversion to organic farming practices. This led to a slight increase in the organically farmed area which stagnated or slightly decreased from 1992 to 1994 (Figure 2.21). In 1993 subsidies for continued organic production were introduced as part of the EU agri-environmental programmes (European Council Regulation 2078/92) – without, however, leading to expansion. Instead, growth was triggered by the entry of FDB, one of the big Danish retail chains, into the organic food business. A large-scale marketing campaign helped to bring a substantial reduction of prices for the consumers. From this time, shelves emptied of bio-products and queues in front of bio-shops were reported. Despite this supply-side push through area payments and price premiums to producers, on the one hand, and the pull through promotion of demand on the other, the organically cultivated area did not increase directly.

A sizeable increase in organically cultivated area was not observed until 1995. In that year, large dairies entered the organic milk market and started to pay an extra subsidy for organic milk in order to cover consumer demand. A price increase of 20 per cent was guaranteed for five years and was also paid during the first two years of conversion. For the dairies, this was a risky decision, as it could not be foreseen whether the marketing of organic milk would be successful economically.

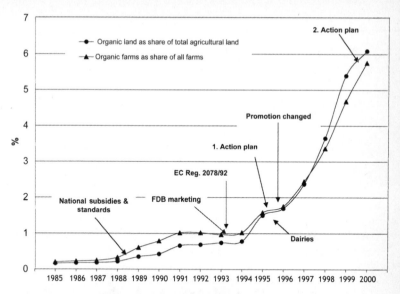

Figure 2.21 The development of organic land area and farms in Denmark (based on Lampkin 2001)

Against this background, the exact formulation of the contracts is of special interest. The contracts specified that a general bonus would be paid if more than 50 per cent of the delivered organic milk was sold as an organic product (bonus model by MD-Foods and Kloever). If this goal was achieved, all milk suppliers received a bonus; however, for organic producers the bonus was somewhat lower than for conventional suppliers. In effect, this was a premium on risk for the conventional farmers.

In the same year (1995) a first national action plan was introduced which had been designed by the National Council for Organic Farming. This council united the organic organisations and a number of other associations, such as the traditional farmers' unions. The action plan was approved virtually unchanged by the Danish government. Aiming to promote organic farming to satisfy the demand, it was very comprehensive and contained a number of recommendations. The entire sector was to be supported. This included supply as well as advice, training, research and above all marketing. Accordingly, only one third of the subsidies for the promotion of organic farming in Denmark was paid directly to the farmers.

The implementation of the action plan was regularly monitored. In 1996 this led to the adjustment of the subsidies as a reaction to an uneven conversion of farm types. In order to extend the range of products and achieve the conversion of diverse farm types, a higher subsidy was paid to arable and pig farms[3] in conversion since 1996 (€410/ha). Accordingly, dairy farms receive a relatively low direct payment, with €141/ha in the first two years of conversion and €80/ha during the third year.

Subsequently, a considerable increase in the organically cultivated area was observed. Despite this substantial increase in subsidies for arable and pig farms, the majority of converting farms were dairy farms – mainly in response to market forces. In the case of pig farms, it is very likely that a fairly strict limitation of livestock density after conversion has restricted the number of converting farms.

In 1999 a second action plan was introduced, this time with the declared goal of reaching a 10 per cent share of the cultivated agricultural area by 2003. Moreover, an export target is given particular prominence. This action plan also included statements such as:

> The current developmental advantage of Denmark for organic products must be used to strengthen the position in the export markets while the barriers for market entry are still low, which means while the export markets are not yet occupied by local suppliers or brands.

This was a reaction to a surplus of organic milk in Denmark; in 2001 approximately 50 per cent of organically produced milk was marketed as conventional milk. The main target export markets are the UK and Germany. This second action plan could have been entitled 'Organic Farming as a Key to Export Markets'. Interestingly, it also attached greater importance to environmental goals as part of the promotion of organic farming. Finally, it contained a number of recommendations aimed at maximising size and specialisation effects without compromising ecological principles. This has led to extensive funding of research projects for the development of practical concepts for cooperation between livestock farmers and stockless farms. This is a good example of the Danish approach to organic farming, which is less ideological than that of other European countries and is based on cooperation between different actors in the area of agriculture.

One important characteristic of the organic farming sector in Denmark which has determined its development is the National Council for Organic Farming. It links the interests of general agriculture with organic farming, as well as taking the interests of consumers, ministries and industrial organisations into account, and thus has contributed to an ongoing discussion process. Another important factor in the development of the sector was the deliberate transfer of the regulation of production standards to national institutions by the organic farming associations as a strategy to gain political influence and save costs.

Sweden

In Sweden organic farming was first supported at the end of the 1980s when the first year of conversion was subsidised. This led to a notable increase in the organically farmed area – followed, however, by stagnation until 1994 (Figure 2.22). In 1993, organic farming associations devised the slogan '10 per cent organic farming by 2000', which was adopted unanimously by the Swedish Parliament in 1994 and triggered an Action Plan 2000 in 1995. This development coincided with Sweden's EU membership, and after 1995 the agri-environmental programmes were implemented as part of Council Regulation 2078/92, with a substantial part of the funding dedicated to organic farming. The number of organically managed farms and the organically managed agricultural area increased substantially, from 50,000 to 300,000 ha.

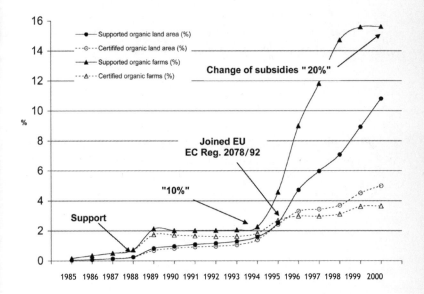

Figure 2.22 The development of organic land area and farms in Sweden (based on Lampkin 2001)

Another important factor in this development was that prices for conventional agricultural products fell substantially after EU accession and the relative profitability of organic farming increased. Good working relations between organic and conventional farming associations were also a positive factor in the development of the sector.[4] By the end of 2000 the organically farmed area had passed the 10 per cent goal set out by the Action Plan 2000 in 1995.

A peculiarity of the promotion of organic farming in Sweden is that farms which are not certified organic (Council Regulation 2092/91) can still be supported.[5] The number of supported organic farms is thus higher than the number of certified organic farms. Many of the supported farms without certification are quite small and cultivate rather marginal sites. For these farms, marketing is of minor importance and certification does not seem worthwhile. The promotion of organic farming in Sweden can therefore be considered as a classic agri-environmental measure pursuing the maintenance and ecologisation of agriculture in marginal areas.

Organic farming support measures in Sweden are characterised by several further peculiarities:

- As in almost all Scandinavian countries, permanent grassland is not granted any area payment within the organic farming support programmes. Permanent grassland plays a minor role in these countries, however, while arable forage or non-permanent grassland is important.

- Supplementary support is granted for arable forage production (clover, clover grass, grass, perennial grassland) if livestock is reared organically. This is an incentive to convert the whole farm.

The original support programme for organic farming was regionalised: higher payments were granted in the high-yielding southern region than in the northern regions. These payments were slightly below the European average and comparable to payments in various German regions.

The new rural development schemes came into effect in 2001 and the organic support scheme was redesigned substantially. Payments are now differentiated by crop, rather than by region. Increased incentives are given to convert the whole farm, including organic livestock husbandry. It will still be possible to convert only partially and still receive some support. However, overall, this will be a less attractive option, in economic terms, than before. Furthermore, the quantitative goal for organic farming was adjusted – '20 per cent organic land area by 2005' – and the total budget for organic support is expected to double by 2005.

Apart from the very obvious positive impact of strategically designed support programmes, several other factors have contributed to the dynamic development of the sector:

- A single label and certification system has ensured consumer confidence in and awareness of organic products.

- Involvement of all major food retailers in distribution of organic food.

- A well-organised organic farming sector and an ongoing discussion process based on a good relationship between the organic and conventional organisations.

- Easy access to advice for organic farming. Advisory services are organised and carried out by the traditional advisory bodies. Cooperation between these bodies and the organic farming movement has always been good.

Italy

Italy is the country with one of the largest organically farmed areas as well as the highest number of organic farms. Organic farming in Italy has developed rapidly since the beginning of the 1990s (Figure 2.23). Individual regions of Italy have developed quite differently: major growth has taken place in the southern regions and on the islands, which altogether account for about 70 per cent of total organic area in Italy. In Italy as much as 6 per cent of the agricultural area is now cultivated organically. In absolute terms, this amounts to more than a million hectares. Remarkably, the share of organically cultivated area and the share of organically managed farms differ greatly. Organic farms are mainly above average in size.

Implementation of European Council Regulation 2092/91 began in 1992 and led to increasing growth. State support for organic farming in Italy was introduced with the implementation of the agri-environmental programmes (Council Regulation 2078/92). This continued for several years as these programmes were implemented in different regions at different times (1993–6). Their influence on the distribution of organic farming is clearly visible, above all in regions with extensive pastures, such as Sardinia, where the subsidies are a welcome additional source of income. In 1998, organic support accounted for 17.5 per cent of total expenditure on the agri-environmental programmes. Although not all certified land has received support under these programmes, the support paid to organic farmers is one of the major causes of Italy's large organic sector.

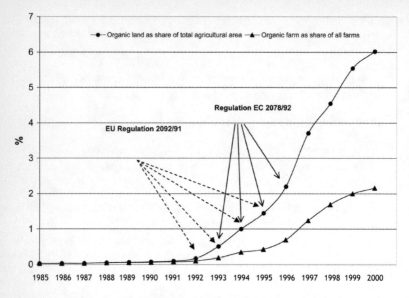

Figure 2.23 The development of organic land area and farms in Italy
(based on Lampkin 2001)

Since a domestic market for organic food did not develop until recently, another important factor for the adoption of organic farming in Italy is the considerable demand for organic products from other countries and the resulting exports. Experts assume that 50 per cent of Italian organic produce is exported: predominantly citrus fruits and vegetables, especially from southern regions such as Sicily, but also olive oil, wine and other specialities. This combination of subsidies and exports seems to have driven the growth of the organic farming sector in Italy so far.

The United Kingdom

The United Kingdom (UK) only recently experienced considerable growth rates in organic farming: before that a long tradition in the sector had led only to a period of stagnation. Implementation of Council Regulation 2092/91 in 1993 resulted in an increase in the conversion of farms. In 1994, support for organic farming was introduced with the implementation of Council Regulation 2078/92 through the Organic Aid Scheme. Payments were quite low, however, and were restricted to conversion. Furthermore, the scheme provided neither higher payment rates for horticulture and fruit production nor maintenance payments for existing organic producers. As a result, it suffered from low uptake rates.

Concern about the low uptake led to the launch of the Organic Conversion Information Service (OCIS) in England and Wales in 1996. This resulted in the conversion of more than 100,000 hectares of land in England by 1999. Between November 1998 and April 1999 in England alone, Soil Association Certification Ltd was receiving applications for producer registration averaging 4,000 hectares per month.

The most significant organic producer cooperative, the Organic Milk Suppliers Cooperative (OMSCO), was established in 1994. The regulations of the Milk Marketing Board, representing all dairy farmers, were lifted and OMSCO was able to take a leading role in market development. By 1997 OMSCO had decoupled the organic milk price from the general milk price through long-term delivery and price contracts. In combination with falling prices for conventional milk, this led to increasing conversion of dairy farms.

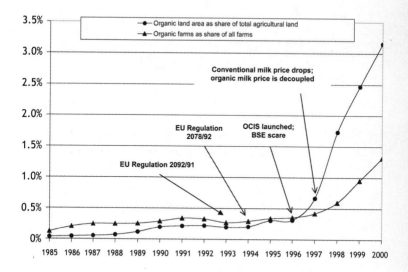

Figure 2.24 The development of organic land area and farms in the UK
(based on Lampkin 2001)

In contrast to most other countries, in the UK organic farming was not perceived as environmentally beneficial. Instead of the integration of the Organic Aid Scheme into the main UK agri-environment programme, a wide range of parallel agri-environmental options was offered. Only a small proportion of the total budget was allocated to the scheme. From 1999 higher conversion payments were introduced – but there were still no maintenance payments for continuing organic production, and budget constraints limited the number of interested farms that could be supported by the scheme.

During the 1990s the BSE crisis and other food scares, and most recently the debate on genetic modification, have led to increased consumer interest and encouraged market actors, such as supermarket chains, to see the organic market as a serious option. As multiple retailers cover approximately 70 per cent of all organic sales in the UK, they play an important role in the development of the organic sector. Safeway was the first supermarket to start selling organic produce in 1981, followed by Sainsbury in 1986 and others in the late 1980s. Today, several of the major multiple retailers have responded to increasing consumer demand by further developing organic product ranges; they expect organics to play an increasingly important role in the general marketing profile of their companies.

Conclusions

This chapter has highlighted the most important characteristics of the organic farming sector in the EU at the dawn of the new millennium. Case studies demonstrate different, individually characterised developments in selected countries. The possibility of drawing a generally valid conclusion from these case studies is limited, but a few observations can be made.

The introduction of subsidies for organic production through the agri-environmental programmes (Council Regulation 2078/92) has helped to increase the organically farmed area and the number of farms. We saw here that variation in the design of subsidies for organic farming greatly influences the actual effect on development of the sector.

Implementation of the common European certification system (Council Regulation 2092/91) in individual countries has paved the way for market segmentation, especially with respect to European trade. National standards have served that purpose at country level.

The involvement of large retailers can help to satisfy consumer demand by overcoming bottlenecks in the processing and distribution chain, and professional promotion by large firms can help to increase consumer consciousness.

Governmental commitment to the organic farming idea through action plans is an important factor in establishing effective support for organic farming. This commitment can be furthered via a well-organised organic farming sector and cooperation with the agricultural establishment.

Although the effect of research on the development of organic farming is not easily measured, further improvement of the organic farming system is necessary, and is a task for research specific to organic farming.

NOTES

1 For results published after this book, see http://www.irs.aber.ac.uk/OMIaRD/ on the research project 'Organic Market Initiatives and Rural Development'.
2 Analysis of the research approach of contributions to the Biannual Organic Farming Research Conference of the German-speaking countries from 1993 to 1999 by Gerber (2001).
3 These farms must have reared pigs at a livestock density of 0.7 to 1.7 livestock units (LU) per hectare, and after conversion livestock density must be between 0.5 and 0.7 LU/ha.
4 Reflecting this cordiality, the president of the conventional farmers' association converted his 800 ha farm to organic management.
5 Control measures are carried out in the same way as for other agri-environmental measures, by taking samples of at least 5 per cent of the participating farms.

CHAPTER 3

Organic farming's contribution to policy objectives

The rapid development of organic farming in the last decade is partly due to increased consideration of its prospects in official policy measures either aimed directly at or having potential application to organic farming.

In the last decade, food quality and minimisation of the negative environmental impacts of agricultural production have gained importance in European agricultural policy. Today, policy makers are striving to achieve the following objectives:

1 minimise negative environmental impacts of agricultural production;

2 provide high-quality food while assuring food supply;

3 preserve both farming incomes and the competitiveness of European agriculture;

4 enhance rural development;

5 reduce expenditure on agriculture in the long term.

Government policies targeting organic farming tend to be controversial. Economists in particular tend to be sceptical about government policy intervention in general as well as measures specifically designed for organic farming. Sound reasons for policies supporting organic farming are therefore increasingly important. In this chapter, the potential contribution of organic farming to some of the stated objectives is discussed.

Environmental performance

The most common argument in support of organic farming is its positive environmental impact. However, selective support for organic practices on

Table 3.1   Impact on the environment: organic compared with conventional farming

(Stolze et al. 2000)

Indicators	+ +	+	0	−	− −
Ecosystem		X			
Floral diversity		X			
Faunal diversity		X			
Habitat diversity			X		
Landscape			X		
Soil		X			
Soil organic matter		X			
Biological activity	X				
Structure			X		
Erosion		X			
Ground and surface water		X			
Nitrate leaching		X			
Pesticides	X				
Climate and air			X		
CO_2		X			
N_2O			X		
CH_4			X		
NH_3		X			
Pesticides	X				
Farm input and output		X			
Nutrient use		X			
Water use			X		
Energy use		X			
Animal health and welfare			X		
Husbandry			X		
Health			X		

Legend: Organic farming performs: ++ much better, + better, 0 the same, − worse, − − much worse than conventional farming; if no data were available, the rating was 0

X   Subjective confidence interval of the final assessment which is marked with X

Box 3.1   Background to the environmental impact of organic farming on the indicator categories given in Table 3.1
(Stolze *et al.* 2000)

Ecosystem indicators: floral and faunal biodiversity, habitat diversity and landscape conservation
Organic farming, because it bans synthetic pesticides and nitrogen fertilisers, performs better than conventional farming with respect to floral and faunal diversity, with secondary beneficial effects on wildlife conservation and landscape. Diverse crop rotations in organic farming provide more habitats for wildlife by supporting a diversity of housing, breeding and nutritional supply. Direct measures for wildlife and biotope conservation, however, depend on the activities of individual farmers. As with any other form of agriculture, organic farming cannot contribute directly to wildlife conservation goals. While research deficits have been identified, it can nevertheless be said that in productive areas it is currently the least detrimental farming system.

Soil indicators: organic matter, biological activity, structure and erosion
Organic farming tends to conserve soil fertility better than conventional farming systems, mainly as a result of higher organic matter content and greater biological activity. Therefore, organic farming seems to control erosion more effectively. A more continuous soil cover due to close crop rotations also supports erosion control. In contrast, no differences between farming systems were identified with regard to soil structure.

Ground and surface water indicators: nitrate leaching and pesticides
Organic farming results in nitrate leaching rates lower than or similar to other farming systems. Leaching rates per hectare are up to 57 per cent lower. However, the leaching rates per tonne of produced output were similar or slightly higher. Ploughing legumes at the wrong time, unfavourable crop rotations, and composting farmyard manure on unpaved surfaces increase the possibility of nitrate leaching in organic farming. However, awareness of the problem and alternative measures have been developed and introduced in practice. The risk of ground and surface water contamination with synthetic pesticides is zero.

Climate and air: CO_2, N_2O, CH_4, NH_3, pesticides
Research on CO_2 emissions shows varying results: on a per-hectare

scale, the CO_2 emissions are 40-60 per cent lower in organic farming systems than in conventional ones, whereas on a per-unit output scale, CO_2 emissions tend to be higher in organic farming systems. Similar results are expected by experts for N_2O and CH_4 emissions, although to date no research results exist. Calculations of NH_3 emissions in organic and conventional farming systems conclude that organic farming bears a lower NH_3 emission potential than conventional farming systems. Nevertheless, housing systems and manure treatment in organic farming should be improved to reduce NH_3 emissions further. Air contamination with synthetic pesticides is significantly lower because the latter are banned under organic standards.

Farm input and output: nutrient, water and energy use

Nutrient balances of organic farms are generally close to zero because organic farms rely heavily on internal nutrient cycling; nitrogen surpluses on organic farms were significantly lower than on conventional farms, since phosphorous and potassium deficits prevail. Energy efficiency of annual and permanent crops seems to be higher in organic farming than in conventional farming, mainly due to lower inputs which require a high (nitrogen) energy input. Research results on water use in organic and conventional farming systems are not available.

Animal health and welfare: husbandry, health

Housing conditions and health status depend highly on farm-specific conditions. Thus in this evaluation the final assessment of housing conditions is that no significant difference exists between organic and conventional farms. This evaluation is in part due to a lack of comparative information. Especially in the cases of poultry and pigs it can be assumed that animal welfare is much higher in organic farming as organic standards specifically take the natural habits of animals into account in relation, for example, to housing systems. Preventive use of synthetic, allopathic medicines is restricted by some national standards and recently also by EU rules. Although the application of homeopathic medicines should be preferred, conventional veterinary measures are permitted and used in acute cases of disease. Health status seems to be closely related to economic relevance of animal husbandry on the farm: significantly fewer incidences of metabolic disorders, udder diseases and injuries were found when dairy production was properly managed. Organic dairy cows tend to have a longer average productive life than conventional dairy cows.

these grounds is only justified if these farming practices actually result in less negative environmental impacts than conventional farming. Obviously, organic farming – like any farming activity – affects the natural environment. However, an extensive analysis of the environmental effects of organic farming compared with conventional farming (Stolze *et al.* 2000) concluded that, on a per hectare scale, organic farming has a less detrimental effect on the environment than conventional systems. This analysis reviewed available evidence relating to the ecosystem, soil, ground and surface water, climate and air, farm input and output, and animal health and welfare, with results that are summarised in Table 3.1.

Poorer performance of organic compared to conventional farming systems was not found in any category. In several categories, organic farming clearly performed better than conventional farming. In two categories (climate and air; animal health and welfare) no clear conclusion could be drawn and the need for further research was identified. Some background on each of the categories is given in Box 3.1.

The issue of genetically modified organisms (GMOs) was not considered in this study in the absence of comprehensive information at the time, despite the relevance of this issue to organic farming and the ban on GMOs under organic standards. The environmental argument against GM seems to be the possibility of gene transfer from GM crops to wild plants and the resulting loss in biodiversity. Furthermore, the effects on living organisms further down the food chain are not yet fully understood and the associated risks therefore cannot be assessed. What is certain is that organic farming remains fundamentally opposed to the use of GMOs in agriculture.

In spite of these clear and broadly positive results, based on a thorough analysis of the literature available in 1999, they require further discussion (Dabbert *et al.* 2000).

- Organic farming seems to perform better with respect to all the indicators considered, but substantial differences exist between the various indicators. Other farming systems, therefore, might have an even less detrimental effect on certain indicators than organic farming. In this respect, we believe that the advantage of organic farming is its broad positive impact on a wide array of environmental indicators, while a mix of specific efforts tackling single indicators is likely to require more effort.

- The relative environmental performance of organic farming differs substantially according to farming system, farm type and region. This makes it difficult to draw general conclusions on this issue and emphasises the need for more information here.

- The results presented might change over time and with developing legislation and policy. For example, organic animal husbandry standards were only defined by EU legislation in 2000 and their effects are not reflected in the above-mentioned results. Thus organic animal husbandry is expected to outperform conventional farming to a greater extent in the future. Equally, tightening of standards for conventional animal husbandry can change this picture. The introduction of new legislation on husbandry of laying hens in Germany is a case in point.

- Linking the environmental effects of agricultural production to farmed area may give a misleading picture. Impact per unit output may be the more appropriate scale on which to evaluate the environmental effects of agricultural production. In that case, organic farming – with lower yields – may under-perform conventional farming. Given sustained surplus production in the EU, however, this argument seems of minor relevance, especially when the issue of keeping marginal land in production is gaining importance.

Although it is difficult to estimate the monetary benefits of the positive environmental contribution made by a farming system, the reverse approach can illustrate these benefits to a certain degree. Attempts have been made to quantify the costs of offsetting negative environmental effects of agricultural production in general. Some of these costs might be avoided by organic farming because this farming system results in less negative environmental effects. Two examples can be cited to highlight this: Waibel and Fleischer (1998) estimated the costs caused by pesticide use in Germany. Pretty *et al.* (2000) assessed the costs caused by negative external effects of agriculture in general in the UK.

In the former Federal Republic of Germany, costs of €125 million per year were estimated for the directly quantifiable effects of pesticides on human health, water quality, residues in food and loss of species. Pretty *et al.* (2000) calculated the annual costs from pesticide contamination of drinking water in the UK to be approximately €190 million per year. Pesticides may be a particularly obvious example of the costly external effects of conventional farming that can be avoided by organic farming. Nonetheless, the example highlights organic farming's potential to reduce the external costs caused by other agricultural production factors.

Box 3.2   Methodological issues in the economic evaluation of the environmental advantages of organic farming

The fact that no market values exist for public goods and externalities is a serious problem. There have been intensive efforts to develop methods to value such externalities in monetary terms; however, 'considerable scepticism still remains regarding the validity and reliability of these methodologies' (Hueth 2002: 32). The consequence is a pragmatic approach which identifies two requirements as being especially important:

- It seems necessary to use a broad set of physical environmental indicators either supplementing monetary values or in addition to them.

- A gradual approach is to be preferred if the (relative) costs of organic farming are to be assessed: rather than asking 'organic *or* conventional?', it seems to be useful to ask 'how much organic, for what purpose, and where?'. This of course implies that marginal thinking becomes important.

In the light of these requirements, it is helpful to look briefly at studies that might have practical relevance for our problem, among them many that have tried to estimate the consequences of a drastic decrease in the use of pesticides (some reviews are Oskam 1997, Kuhl *et al*. 2001, Waibel and Fleischer 2002). The results of such studies tend to show quite substantial costs if no pesticides are used. As Waibel and Fleischer (2001: 12) point out:

> All existing studies on drastic pesticide scenarios, no matter if a partial or a general equilibrium is used, come to the same conclusion: They state that on average, the benefits of pesticides outweigh their costs. Such a result is not surprising, simply because two extreme scenarios are compared: the current situation versus a complete pesticide ban or an extremely high reduction.... This definitely limits the usefulness of all these studies with regard to policy conclusions.

By their very nature, these studies concentrate on pesticide (and sometimes nitrogen fertiliser) use, so they also fall short of the first requirement.

The findings of studies that explicitly look at the cost of a widespread conversion have been reviewed by Offermann (2000):

> In spite of large differences in methods used and regions covered, all studies show a significant, and remarkably similar reduction in the

➡

production of most agricultural products, with the decline in output being highest for cereals, pig and poultry. The development of farm income is to a large extent dependent on the assumed prices, and can be both higher and lower than in the respective reference scenarios. (Offermann 2000: 2).

Offermann notes serious methodological limitations in most studies because they were not able to model a limited area conversion endogenously, let alone the resulting changes in organic prices. Impacts on conventional markets are often neglected as well. In addition, even when environmental indicators have been included in these studies, they have been considered only to a limited extent.

In summary, much of the literature that is potentially useful for assessing the environmental costs and benefits of organic farming does not meet either of the two key requirements outlined above. This was one of the motivations for the extensive literature review on the physical effects of organic farming presented earlier in this chapter.

There are many studies potentially relevant to the evaluation of the environmental benefits and costs of organic farming. Some of the considerable methodological problems that arise in this area are highlighted in Box 3.2.

Food quality

Although food quality can be considered a private good, many governments have included the provision of food safety in their policy objectives. Extensive reviews of existing research findings on the physically measurable quality of organically produced food compared with conventionally produced food (Woese *et al.* 1995; Stolze *et al.* 2000) have shown that no firm conclusions about the quality of organically produced food in general can be drawn (Table 3.2) in the absence of adequate results from comparative investigations of organic as opposed to conventionally produced food, although for some of the indicators organic food performed better than its conventional equivalent. As expected, the risk of contamination with pesticides and nitrates was found to be lower in organic food.

With regard to animal produce, no comparative investigations exist that prove the higher quality of organic produce. However, many research

Table 3.2 The quality of organic and conventionally produced food (Stolze *et al.* 2000)

Indicators	+ +	+	O	–	– –
Food quality		X			
Pesticide residues	X				
Nitrate		X			
Mycotoxins			X		
Heavy metals			X		
Desirable substances			X		
BSE risk		X			
Antibiotic residues	X				

Legend: Organic farming performs: ++ much better, + better, o the same, – worse, – – much worse than conventional farming; if no data were available, the rating was o.

X   Subjective confidence interval of the final assessment which is marked with X

findings have highlighted the risks associated with conventional animal produce. For example, the risk of antibiotic residues is assumed to be lower in organically produced meat since sub-therapeutic application of antibiotics is strictly forbidden, while therapeutic use is avoided as far as possible and strictly controlled. The discussion of BSE-contaminated meat and the risk to humans also suggests a somewhat lower risk associated with organic compared with conventional meat. This is due to a long-time ban on animal meals in feed and the exclusive use of animals from a controlled origin as far as possible. Nevertheless, BSE can also occur in organic herds.

Thus there are risks associated with conventionally produced food that are less likely to apply to organically produced food. Especially when exercising the precautionary principle in relation to food safety and agriculture, organic farming seems to be a viable option. This view is confirmed by a European Commission summary report on this issue (Box 3.3).

Another argument in favour of organic food is the ban on GMOs by organic standards. On the one hand, the effects of GMOs on humans are not fully understood, but consumers are afraid of the effects of unknown genetic elements in food and their possible impact (allergic reactions, for

Box 3.3   The European Commission's view on food quality and food safety issues in organic farming (EC 2002a)

Food safety

It is not possible to claim that organic food is safer than non-organic food, since all food products sold in the EU must fulfil the same strict criteria on food safety. The risk of contamination of food with pesticides and nitrates has, however, been found to be lower in food produced organically.

Both organic and non-organic food products are sometimes (but not always) analysed for residues of pesticides. However, organic food is tested more often since the food authorities and organic inspection bodies both carry out tests on it. Depending on the type of product, pesticide residue is sometimes also found in food labelled as organic. It should however be noted that, even if all the regulations have been adhered to, it is still possible for an organic product to be contaminated with pesticides, for instance by the drifting of pesticides from a neighbouring field. However, it is unusual to find residues in organic food and when they are found they are at lower levels.

The risk of discovering antibiotic residues is assumed to be lower in organically produced meat, since the preventive application of antibiotics is strictly forbidden and therapeutic use is avoided as far as possible.

The use of manure as a potential source of fertilisation should not pose particular problems in organic farming. It is also commonly used in non-organic farming and should not pose any particular problems with microbial contamination if carried out according to good practices ....

A pilot project on food quality has been launched by the Directorate-General for Health and Consumer Protection. This project aims to assess the overall quality of organic and non-organic food currently available on the European market. The preliminary results mainly confirm the above findings. Only a small percentage of organic produce analysed contained pesticide residues and the detected residues levels mostly ranged below the legal limits. The study also showed a lower number of different pesticides found in organic food. It is sometimes claimed that the risk of contamination with mycotoxins is higher in organic food. The study could not confirm this. Differences in vitamins and mineral contents were observed, with the organic produce representing the higher levels in most cases. However, these differences were not significant. Moreover, the organic food showed lower concentrations of nitrate.

➡️

> ### Food quality
> Taste and appearance are matters of personal judgement and this, of course, is something that has to be left to the individual consumer, often according to cultural or other factors. Recognising that there are already many flavour variations between different fruits and vegetables depending on the variety, the degree of ripeness, freshness or length of storage, objective judgements are often difficult.
>
> Some studies have found a higher content of dry matter, minerals, vitamins and flavour-providing 'phyto-nutrients' in organic products, especially in green vegetables, and a lower concentration of potentially harmful nitrate. Other studies have been unable to confirm this, however.

example). On the other hand, if a market for non-GMO products is maintained, crop varieties that might be displaced are conserved. A trend in this direction can already be observed independently of the GMO issue. Organic farming generally relies more on traditional varieties of crops as these tend to be adapted to the non-pesticide, non-fertiliser environment of organic farming systems. This may contribute to the preservation of certain species and variety in food culture.

Consumers buy organic food and are willing to pay higher prices, mostly because they are convinced that organic food is of higher quality. In other words, they believe it tastes better and/or that it is safer, less harmful or healthier than conventional food.

Farm income

One of the main concerns of agricultural policy is to preserve the economic viability of farming in general and ensure incomes high enough to keep farming families in the sector. A comparative review of the economic situation of organic and conventional farms in Europe up to 2000 (Offermann and Nieberg 2000) shows that average profits are similar, with nearly all organic farms achieving +/– 20 per cent of the profits achieved by the relevant conventional reference groups (Figure 3.1). On the one hand, the economic performance of organic farms in comparison to conventional farms strongly depends on the level of support payments for organic farming and the type of Common Agricultural Policy measures employed, such as set-aside or compensatory arable payments. Support

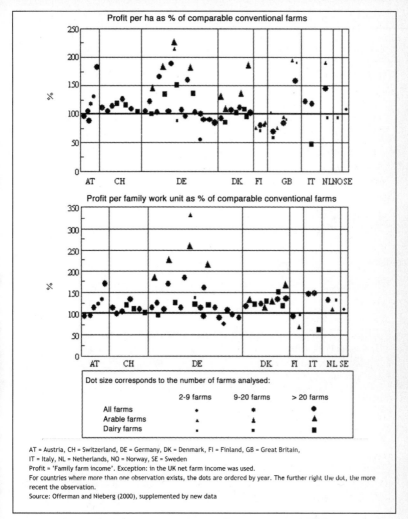

Figure 3.1   Profits of organic farms relative to comparable conventional farms in different countries: results of different studies, 1992–2000

payments to organic farming are intended to compensate for yield losses due to production restrictions in organic farming. As mentioned in Chapter 1, the advantage of organic farming is that part of the losses due to lower yields is compensated for by the price premiums that consumers are willing to pay.

For the same reasons, economic performance differs significantly between organic farms – substantially depending on farm type and country. The difference between countries is highlighted in Table 3.3, which shows case studies of typical dairy farms from various countries. Not only is the typical production structure quite different, but national factors such as land rents significantly influence profitability. The most prominent example, however, is the effect of a difference in support for organic production. At the time of the research, the UK did not pay any organic aid to farms beyond conversion. In the cases presented, this is reflected in the share of profits (0.33 per cent) from organic support payments (see also Offermann and Nieberg 2000).

Table 3.3   Typical organic dairy farms in selected EU countries in 1999 (Häring 2001)

	UK	Germany	Denmark	Italy
Total UAA[1] (ha)	59	55	66	42
of which arable	56%	48%	100%	100%
Dairy cows	62	38	60	28
Total LU[2]/ha UAA	1.3	1.1	1.4	0.9
FCM (kg)	5 583	5 062	6 672	5 170
AWU[3]/100 ha year	2.6	3.7	2.1	5.9
Rent price arable land (€/ha)	759	460	430	207
Profit from subsidies (all)	5%	75%	37%	34%
Profit from organic aid	0%	33%	22%	29%

[1] Utilisable agricultural area
[2] Livestock unit
[3] Agricultural work unit

These results are not unexpected. As long as farm income is a major factor for the decision to convert, and conversion is voluntary, conversion to organic farming is a sensible option for those likely to earn a similar or higher profit. Obviously, the income effect of conversion to organic production depends on farm type, location and country. Generally, extensive farms in marginal regions are more likely to benefit from conversion than intensive farms in fertile regions (Chapter 1).

Rural development

Rural development has become a key issue in European agricultural policy, and a range of policies has been implemented to enhance rural areas, with the objective of increasing the income of rural households and reducing unemployment rates. Employment in agriculture is already low in rural areas in the EU, and is expected to decline further, as in many areas farms are still too small to benefit from economies of scale.

An argument often used to support organic farming is the observation that, on average, organic farming requires a higher labour input than conventional farming and engages more in processing and marketing. For example, Offermann and Nieberg (2000) found labour input on organic farms in Germany and Switzerland to be an average 20 per cent higher than on comparable conventional farms, mainly reflecting a substitution of chemical inputs by labour and a higher proportion of labour-intensive activities (Figure 3.2). Additionally, organic farms tend to employ more paid labour while relying less on family workers.

However, considering the small workforce employed in agriculture (Figure 3.3) and the size of the organic farming subsector, only minor effects are expected. For example, in a region where agricultural employment

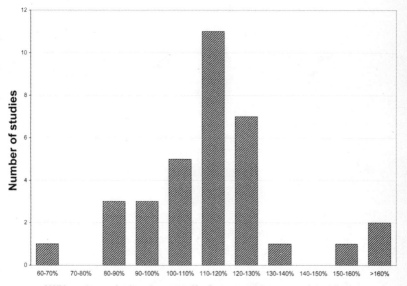

Figure 3.2   Agricultural work units per hectare of utilisable agricultural area on organic and comparable conventional farms: results of various studies (Offermann and Nieberg 2000)

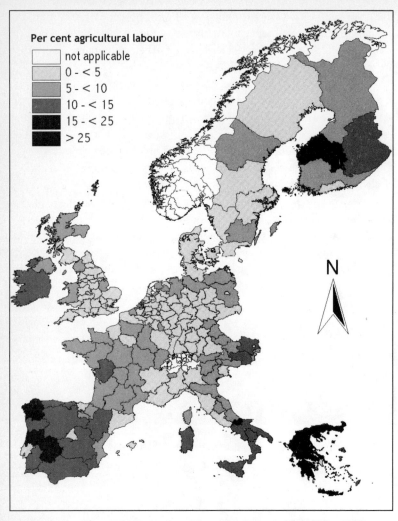

Figure 3.3   Share of labour force in agriculture in the EU in 1995
(Eurostat 1999)

accounts for 5 per cent of all jobs, a 20 per cent increase in organic farming would result in a mere 0.2 per cent increase in overall employment, despite the higher labour input in organic farming. The expected direct contribution of organic farming to rural employment rates is therefore insignificant, but other indirect factors might contribute to rural development.

First, marketing and processing of organic products to date have mainly developed as small businesses closely related to primary organic production but legally independent. Many of these are efforts by farm families to create additional income sources for increasingly redundant family labour; others have evolved from cooperative initiatives, often creating employment opportunities in the long run. Such clusters of organic agribusiness firms, working and networking together, can create an additional dynamic in developing the sector.

Second, organic farming might contribute to a positive image of rural areas, of benefit not only to agriculture but also to other sectors of rural economies. Young farmers increasingly seem to favour organic farming (Tress 2000, for example), and the conversion to organic farming could be a reason for them to remain in farming instead of choosing other employment opportunities. A strong commitment to environmental goals might add to the appeal of a region for tourism, which is very likely to have positive effects when companies from other sectors choose a certain region as a business location. As a result, several regions exist which have tried to use the positive image created by organic farming as a motor for rural development (Biosphärenreservat Rhön in Germany is an example).

In short, although organic farming is expected to have little direct effect on unemployment rates in rural areas, small-scale marketing and processing initiatives may contribute directly to rural employment. Indirect effects such as increased employment in tourism due to the positive 'ecological' image of a region can also be of importance.

Surplus reduction and government expenditure

The Common Agricultural Policy is one of the European Union's main sources of expenditure. For the planning period of Agenda 2000 (2000–6), a projected €300 billion will be spent (EC 2000a), more than half of the whole budget. Traditionally, the two major sources of expenditure have been direct payments to producers, and market support such as export subsidies and storage costs. With the objective of reducing storage costs and stabilising market prices, surplus reduction itself has become a declared policy goal.

Organic farming can contribute significantly to surplus reduction since the observed yields are much lower in organic as compared to conventional production. This is particularly true of plant production (Offermann and Nieberg 2000). For example, cereal yields in organic production are typically only 60–70 per cent of those from conventional production, although comparative yield levels vary with country, region and crop. Unlike most organic crops, organic vegetable yields tend to be as high as conventional yields. While performances in livestock production are similar to those of conventional production, the lower stocking densities observed on organic farms result in lower performance per hectare.

Direct payments within the agri-environmental programmes are the main source of expenditure on organic farming, amounting to €300 million for the 15 EU countries in 1996 (Lampkin *et al.* 1999a). This volume is often quoted by critics of organic farming. However, taking only costs related to the above-mentioned reduction of surpluses and change in farming structure after conversion to organic farming into account, expenditure would be reduced approximately by half of the amount spent on direct subsidies (Zanoli and Gambelli 1999). This emerges from a comparison of the hypothetical situation of Europe without organic farming (0 per cent) with the observed situation in 1997. A similar calculation reported by Offermann (2000) puts the savings in arable area and headage payments under Agenda 2000 conditions at 13 per cent of the expenses for organic farming. Obviously, an increase in organic farming area would still result in higher expenditure than for conventional agriculture, but compared with other agri-environmental schemes, the previously mentioned benefits might become increasingly important in the future.

Criticism of organic farming policy

The potential benefits of organic farming to current EU agricultural policy objectives have been discussed in the previous sections. Nevertheless, organic farming is not beyond criticism. Such criticism has to be taken seriously. Organic farming policy is often discussed in specific contexts created by current daily political events – and, of course, these contexts influence the way arguments are made. We discuss the most important criticism below, and assess whether it is justified.

Criticism from agricultural economists

In 2001, after the BSE crisis hit Germany and following the resignations of the Minister of Agriculture and the Minister of Health, the consumer protection portfolio was transferred from the Ministry of Health to the Ministry of Agriculture. A new Consumer Protection Minister was appointed and the new Minister of Agriculture set out to 'transform agricultural policy'. Part of this proclaimed change was a stronger focus on environmental issues in agriculture, accompanied by a positive attitude towards organic farming. This prompted an attack on organic farming and its underlying rationale by 42 German professors of agricultural economics – a solid two thirds majority of their profession within Germany – in a joint statement demanding a rational policy for agriculture (FAZ 2001). In essence, they argued that the government should not intervene in favour of organic farming.

These are their most important theses:

- Organic farming does not prevent BSE.

- Small and organic – a dead end.

- Existing programmes supporting organic farming are not even fully utilised.

- Consumers do not wish to support organic farming.

- Financial support of organic farming leads to decreasing price premiums for organic products and to organic farming's permanent dependency on state hand-outs.

- Conventional farming can provide the same public goods as organic farming but at less cost.

- Government intervention distorts competition: it must be abolished and must not just undergo a change in intentions and objectives.

'Organic farming does not prevent BSE'
In a strictly technical sense, organic farming does not have a zero BSE risk (see p. 74 above). Other means of dealing with the causes of BSE are probably much cheaper than a conversion to organic farming. Moreover, support for organic farming is certainly no substitute for strict controls on feedstuffs. Up to this point the argument is valid. However, the question is whether the technical view is sufficient to analyse a political crisis of a wider dimension.

For example, in Germany the BSE crisis proved to be a catalytic event. The public suddenly realised that agricultural policy spends a lot of money without supplying the goods demanded by the general public, such as animal welfare or food safety. Organic farming seems to come off well in this respect – as we have shown in a previous section.

'Small and organic – a dead end'
Organic farms are not necessarily smaller than conventional farms. Farm size depends primarily on historical and regional factors: in East Germany, for example, very large organic farms have existed for more than a decade (Stolze 1998). Although some proponents of organic farming have considered efficient farm organisation contrary to the idea of organic farming, organic farms are subject to the same pressure to adapt to changing external conditions as conventional farms. This often has similar structural consequences, such as growth. Organic farms also take advantage of economies of scale. However, it is not size which defines an organic farm, but its method of production.

'Existing programmes supporting organic farming are not even fully utilised'
This is interpreted as a lack of interest in organic farming, implying that there is no need to support it. Indeed, in some regions, support payments for organic farming were not significantly higher than those for integrated farming. However, it must be remembered that the restrictions with which organic farmers must comply are much more demanding and more costly than those required by other farming systems, and this is why not many farms have converted. Since the design of the agri-environmental programmes which support organic farming set the bar so high, it is not surprising that support programmes have not been fully utilised.

'Consumers do not wish to support organic farming'
Evidence supports the hypothesis that potential demand for organic food is much higher than the currently realised demand. The obstacles to realising higher demand have been identified clearly. Obviously, this claim neglects the fact that consumers are not forced to buy organic products but are free to choose organic or conventional products.

'Financial support of organic farming leads to decreasing price premiums for organic products and to organic farming's permanent dependency on state handouts'
An increase in organic farming area due to direct subsidies for and increased profitability of organic farms may result in an erosion of price premiums. This argument holds as long as demand is consolidated. However, if the 'bottleneck' theory described earlier applies and part of the potential demand can be realised – by political measures, for example – then price premiums can be sustained in the short to medium term. In the

long term, price premiums may erode. At present, however, several options exist to avoid erosion of price premiums – without price support measures. Nevertheless, it is important to consider whether direct subsidies are the appropriate measure to support organic farming.

'Conventional farming can provide the same public goods as organic farming but at less cost'
Measures aimed at achieving specific public goods, such as environmental objectives, within conventional farming, may be more effective than subsidies to organic farming by providing the same benefits at lower cost. This might be true if a small, one-dimensional environmental problem is to be addressed. The more aspects have to be taken into account, however, the more expensive specific measures are to administer – an argument in favour of organic farming.

Yet comprehensive research results comparing both the physical and cost effects of organic and conventional farming on a broad base do not exist. In part, this lack of clear evidence reflects the fact that the results depend strongly on the types of public goods targeted, the type of farms involved, and regional aspects.

'Government intervention distorts competition: it must be abolished and must not just undergo a change in intentions and objectives'
Economists tend to be sceptical about government policy intervention in the market. They often argue that policy intervention is established to benefit a specific social group with an effective lobby. This often takes place at the expense of other groups and decreases overall social welfare. But even these 'free market' economists have developed a theoretical framework with scope for state intervention in the market; this is known as 'economic welfare theory'. A fundamental argument against organic farming policy – or, indeed, any support policy – is that it hinges on efficiency considerations and that government intervention impedes competitive market equilibrium.

Critics of a purely 'free market' approach to official policy also need to take a closer look at the arguments provided by the theoretical framework of welfare theory. With respect to organic farming, the following questions are relevant:

- Can the potential contributions of organic farming to official policy objectives fit into that framework?

- Can instruments demanded by supporters of organic farming fit into that framework?

If they do and could actually be supported by a generally free-market-oriented, liberal approach to policy, quite strong arguments in favour of political support for organic farming arise.

Justification for intervention in favour of organic farming

A variety of factors can impede market functions (see, for example, Henrichsmeyer and Witzke 1994). Four important factors are discussed in more detail:

- Markets do not function properly owing to the nature of goods involved, such as public goods.

- Markets may lead to an income distribution within society which is considered unacceptable.

- A lack of information severely impedes market functions.

- The negative effects of earlier government intervention on markets need to be corrected and eased by new intervention.

Public goods

The first and most important one is the issue of public goods.

> A common, collective or public good is defined here as any good such that, if any person ... in a group ... consumes it, it cannot feasibly be withheld from others in that group. (Olson 1965)

Examples of these goods include a secure national defence or clean air. To provide goods like these (or to avoid public ills like dirty air), governments must overcome the logic of collective action, which says that people have very little incentive to organise politically and to work for the provision of public goods. If the good is provided, people cannot be excluded from enjoying it, whether they worked collectively with others to produce the good or not.

According to welfare theory, a competitive market will produce an optimal quantity of private goods. However, it will not produce adequate quantities of pure public goods, given their above-mentioned nature. Such market failure results in a loss of social welfare.

Biodiversity is an example of a public good. The knowledge that bio-diversity is enhanced by a specific agricultural system might actually increase many people's utility. However, it is difficult to exclude anyone from the use of biodiversity. As humans are assumed to act solely in self-interest, they use as much of that public good as they desire. Consequently, this good (biodiversity) becomes scarce at some point, and demand would outstrip supply.

Imagine a single person giving half of her income to a project support-ing biodiversity. For that person, this would be a major sacrifice. However, the overall situation of biodiversity would hardly change. In contrast, some kind of collective action can help to overcome this situation at little expense to individuals. One option of collective action is government intervention. For large-scale problems, government intervention is partic-ularly appropriate.

In the case of organic farming, it means that if this farming system provides more public goods than other farming systems, government inter-vention can be justified if organic farming is the cheapest way to produce the goods desired.

Income distribution
As we have seen, because of the nature of public goods, their allocation within a society tends to be sub-optimal. However, market effects can also lead to a sub-optimal distribution income. Correction of a sub-optimal income distribution is therefore a common objective of government actions. For example, in most countries, income taxes are proportionally higher – in theory – for high incomes than for low incomes.

One of the objectives of European agricultural policy is to improve farmers' incomes. Another important objective is regional development, especially increasing jobs in disadvantaged and rural areas with high unemployment rates. Therefore, if organic farming can contribute to improving farmers' incomes, the agricultural sector's income, rural develop-ment and the job situation in marginal areas, government intervention is justified.

Market transparency
A third justification of government intervention is a lack of market transparency due to inadequate information for both the consumer and the producer. A lack of market transparency can result in market failure and sub-optimal provision of goods.

In the organic sector, consumers may not be informed adequately about the attributes of organic products, and this may influence their decision to consume organic products. For consumers, relevant information on organic food may include the quality of organic food, details of organic farming practices – the fact that conversion to organic production takes two to three years, for example – and specifics of marketing organic produce.

For consumers, a lack of transparency represents increased risk. Consumers' aversion to risk may thus result in sub-optimal demand for organic goods. Ideally, the quality of different products can be easily distinguished at the point of sale by labelling (compare Darby and Karny 1973; Nelson 1970). Many regulations and labels therefore exist within the food market. Once the consumers have bought their food, they can experience characteristics like freshness or taste. Other characteristics are not immediately apparent, but are nonetheless important, such as the presence of undesirable substances which only affect health in the long run. These are called 'credence characteristics' because consumers have to believe in these characteristics – there is no way to check for them.

This is an important aspect of organic food. Consumers cannot distinguish directly whether a product is organic or not. As explained in previous sections, the EU has implemented a certification and control system for organic food that guarantees its genuine organic origin/production. In reality, however, finding organic products and distinguishing them from conventional products is still difficult. Many consumers still do not buy organic food because they do not trust that it is actually organic. This situation can justify government intervention. Market function and economic efficiency can be improved if consumers can distinguish more easily between organic and conventional food and trust is established.

For producers, information on actual market prices and qualities, as well as information on expected trends in consumer preferences and future price levels, may be most relevant.

Correction of previous intervention
Some of the justification of government intervention discussed is more a theoretical guideline than a real-world practice. Much of the agricultural policy in force in Europe today does not fulfil such strict criteria. For such situations, a 'second-best solution' approach has been developed. In such cases government interventions are justified if they ease market distortions caused by previous government interventions. An example could be support of organic farming because of its contribution to reducing surplus

production and thus cutting down on government expenditure in the EU.

Thus there are arguments that can justify government intervention in favour of organic farming. Even in welfare theory this type of intervention is not ruled out *per se*. However, this does not resolve the matter of which measures are best. State support of organic farming is certainly not the only means to reach the objectives discussed in this chapter. We believe, however, that support of organic farming can play a role in a portfolio of government policy measures that also target conventional farmers to a certain degree.

Such a portfolio of policies may consist of economic approaches (such as taxes and subsidies), regulatory approaches (forbidding certain practices), and moral persuasion, in which politicians try to change opinions and actions. All of these have specific advantages and disadvantages. Environmental subsidies, for example, can affect low-income groups more than high-income groups. Regulations must be enforced or they tempt people to ignore them. Moral persuasion often remains unheard. Practical politics often consists of several measures – to avoid the serious side-effects that may flow from single measures.

The political appeal of policies in support of organic farming lies among other things in the multifunctional effects achieved by this instrument; more than one objective can be reached at the same time. This also poses a tremendous challenge to economists charged with analysing and evaluating the effects of such policies compared with the alternatives.

Conclusions

In this chapter, we have adopted an approach to policy evaluation that takes the actual and proclaimed objectives of politicians as the starting point for our analysis. For the purpose of discussing organic farming policies, we see at least four potentially relevant positions (Dabbert 2000), explained in Box 3.4.

The chosen approach is rational because it is based on the assumption that policy objectives and instruments are closely linked. It is critical because it does not assume that organic farming has a value in itself: instead, its advantages and disadvantages are carefully assessed. It is transparent because it is based on easily comprehensible objectives voiced by politicians, and looks at whether these can be achieved or not.

For policy design, however, it is not only the relative contribution of organic farming, compared with conventional farming, to policy objectives

Box 3.4   Possible positions on agricultural policy (Dabbert 2000)

1 Politicians' actual or proclaimed objectives are the starting point for policy analysis. The aim of such analysis is to identify political measures best suited to achieve these objectives, which might include generating farm income, securing the food supply, or promoting environmentally friendly agricultural practices. In this context, organic farming is viewed as one way to achieve these objectives which competes with others. Policies which influence the organic farming sector have to be compared with other policies in order to determine the extent to which they contribute to policy objectives. The policy mix that achieves a specific objective at least cost is considered the best. This is the traditional approach to policy evaluation.

2 Stated or actual policy objectives might not reflect the interests of the general public. In an attempt to stay in office or increase votes, politicians may pursue objectives which do not necessarily help to maximise the welfare of society. With respect to organic farming, it is therefore necessary to assess whether policies supporting organic farming actually increase social welfare. The difficulty of this approach is to find an operational definition of social welfare. Nevertheless, this is the approach most commonly pursued by economists when assessing policies.

3 An increase in the scope of organic farming is considered a policy objective in itself. The advantages of organic farming have been demonstrated and are accepted. The only remaining question is how to increase the scale of organic farming most effectively. Accordingly, political measures are analysed solely in terms of their contribution to the further development of organic farming. This is a legitimate standpoint maintained by organic farming interest groups.

4 All three preceding views clearly distinguish between objectives and instruments. However, they often fail to describe policy design in reality. Actual policy-making process does not necessarily follow such a procedure; problems and policies 'have lives of their own' (Kingdon 1995: 201). Only under special circumstances ('policy windows') are measures (such as support of organic farming) attached to problems. For example, the BSE crisis in Germany prompted a change in agricultural policy towards organic farming support, probably not the most effective measure to deal with BSE. Furthermore, BSE avoidance had never been on the agenda of organic farming. In contrast to the preceding views of agricultural policy, objectives on the one hand and political measures to achieve these objectives on the other are not differentiated. This policy view of actual politics is useful, although it contributes little to policy design.

which is relevant. The main issue is the absolute contribution of an activity to certain policy objectives at relatively lower costs than those caused by an alternative activity.

The existence of public goods justifies and necessitates government intervention. Based on the information available to date, no clear conclusion can be drawn that organic farming achieves the desired effects at lower costs than other farming activities. Despite a certain 'auto-funding' rate through reduction of public expenditure, critics argue that costs of direct payments to organic farming are extremely high and that the same targets could be reached more cost-effectively via other, more specific measures (Alvensleben 1998). This leads directly to the question of the required quantity and variety of such measures to be implemented to achieve the same effects on such a wide array of targets as organic farming, and of the costs of their implementation, administration and control. It is therefore concluded that organic farming can contribute to several of the stated policy objectives of the CAP. While it can be argued that an improvement in a broad set of indicators achieved by organic farming might be more cost-effective than other farming systems, the empirical information on this issue is scarce. Nevertheless, the positive effects on a broad range of official policy objectives justify the support of organic farming.

Even if analysis goes beyond the contributions to current stated policy objectives, organic farming support may be justified as necessary to correct negative effects of earlier government intervention or because a lack of information is severely impeding market functions. The empirical situation presented in Chapter 2, especially the 'immature nature' of the organic sector, justifies support for organic farming. However, in the past a very narrow definition of government instruments in support of organic farming seemed to prevail, with arguments focusing on direct financial support to farms while neglecting the wide range of other possible instruments. Yet organic farming support is not necessarily a protectionist policy. Currently, the organic market is probably among the least protected: market intervention for organic farming does not exist. A non-protectionist policy in support of organic farming is possible. For example, a clear policy on standards, certification and labelling can favour both trade and the development of organic farming.

Arguments in favour of or against organic farming depend on the political and economic situation. Major political developments will also influence what constitute sensible policies with respect to organic farming. We thus turn to the changing policy environment.

CHAPTER 4

A changing policy environment

The agricultural policy environment has changed rapidly over the past ten years and continues to do so. The high expenditure on current agricultural policies is not coherent with the objective of the European Commission and the national governments to reduce expenditure on agriculture. EU enlargement will put further pressure on budgets.

Policy makers seem quite keen to consider organic farming as a policy instrument, especially when targeting the following issues:

- environmental degradation;

- maintaining marginal land in production;

- farmers' incomes;

- surplus production and the negative impacts of agriculture on international commodity markets.

Significant price premiums as a result of increasing demand for organic products have helped policy makers to support organic farming. Policies targeting organic farming directly have been discussed in Chapter 2 (pp. 42–54). However, organic farming and any policy supporting it cannot be considered in isolation within the current EU policy framework. In this chapter we therefore discuss the impacts of general policy developments on organic farming in particular:

- the framework offered by the new EU Common Agricultural Policy, Agenda 2000;

- the opportunities and threats deriving from the enlargement of the EU through the accession of Central and Eastern European countries;

- the negotiation of the WTO agreements on agricultural trade.

Agenda 2000

Agenda 2000, agreed upon in March 1999, is the most recent drastic reform of the EU Common Agricultural Policy (EC 1999b). Reforms realised in Agenda 2000 are better understood in view of the history of the CAP since the 1950s. In that decade the Common Agricultural Policy was designed against the backdrop of famine and food shortage in the war and postwar years. Thus an increase in productivity was its main objective. Policy makers also envisaged a fair income for farmers and aimed to establish a system of stable prices for agricultural products.

Government interventions, implemented step by step for most agricultural products in Europe, turned out to be a great success. Guaranteed prices and sales led to a rise in production. Food security was assured and price fluctuations were limited. But this success was short-lived: farmers reacted to the new conditions and, taking full advantage of technological progress, began to produce more than markets could absorb. Despite several smaller reforms in the 1980s, surpluses reached a level at which drastic reform became inevitable.

The most important reform in the history of the CAP came in 1992 when McSharry was agricultural commissioner. Prices were reduced drastically for several important product groups. To counter the negative impact on agricultural incomes, compensation payments – headage or area payments – were introduced for farmers. For the first time funds for agri-environmental measures were made available. Their financial profile was minor, but their existence strategically important. The significance for organic farming of these 'accompanying measures', introduced in 1992, was discussed in Chapter 2 (pp. 42–3).

EU enlargement and international demands within World Trade Organisation (WTO) negotiations for a liberalisation of EU agricultural policy required further reform at the end of the last century: Agenda 2000. The agricultural reforms which are part of Agenda 2000 continue and consolidate changes introduced by earlier reforms. Their main objectives are:

- to increase the competitiveness of EU agricultural products on the domestic and world markets;

- to integrate environmental and structural considerations more fully with the implementation of the CAP;

- to ensure a fair income for farmers;

- to simplify agricultural legislation and decentralise its application;

- to improve food safety;

- to strengthen the EU position in the new round of WTO negotiations;

- to stabilise agricultural spending in real terms at its 1999 level.

Agricultural expenditure was still 51 per cent of the overall EU financial framework for 2000. Expenditure on the structural policy measures and rural development (including measures such as agri-environmental provisions, an early retirement scheme, compensatory payments and reforestation) is, on average, just above 10 per cent of the total yearly budget for the years 2000–6. Expenditure on market support measures will make up 89 per cent of total CAP expenditure in the same period.

The Rural Development Regulation (Council Regulation 1257/99) (EC 1999c) has been added to the Agenda 2000 package for agriculture. This 'second pillar' of the CAP is designed with the objective of securing the future of the Community's rural areas by promoting:

- the accompanying measures introduced in 1992 (early retirement, agri-environmental provisions, forestry);

- measures to diversify agricultural holdings (support for processing and marketing of agricultural products, training, promotion, diversification of agriculture, etcetera);

- structural adaptation of holdings and measures to keep young people in rural areas and farming;

- the inclusion of these measures in Rural Development Plans devised by member states and approved, together with the other accompanying measures set out in the 1992 reform, by the European Commission (these plans, intended to simplify agricultural legislation and decentralise its application, are innovative in integrating various policy instruments better and enhancing synergies among different measures).

However, the total budget of the CAP (in real terms) is 'frozen' at its 1999 level. Thus, for agri-environmental provisions, competition for financial resources is greater. Accordingly, organic farming has to compete with other environmental and rural development measures, especially if the demand for direct conversion support increases in line with past trends. This applies to farmers considering conversion to organic farming as well as established organic farmers whose five-year agri-environmental commitments have expired or will expire (Lampkin and Midmore 2000). In some countries, the stricter financial framework of Agenda 2000 has already impacted on the growth of the organic sector by frustrating new converters' expectations of income support.

Furthermore, a stronger focus on the principle of subsidiarity with more decentralised policy and decision making may introduce further differences among member states and/or regions within such member states. This may have unforeseeable effects on the development of organic farming and the cohesion of the sector itself.

Nevertheless, within mainstream agricultural measures, part of the funding for direct payments will be allocated to 'national envelopes' which may be distributed by member states according to local needs. Resources from these national envelopes could be used to support particular production systems, such as organic beef production (Lampkin and Midmore 2000).

The continuing shift from price support to direct area and headage support payments tends to benefit organic farmers because of the lower yields in organic farming (Häring 2001). However, price reductions for conventional products also affect prices for organic products. For organically produced milk farmers usually receive the price of conventional milk plus a price premium. In this respect Agenda 2000 is likely to have negative impacts on organic farming.

In July 2002 the European Commission published its mid-term review of the Agenda 2000 framework (EC 2002b). This Commission paper proposed a number of far-reaching changes to the CAP framework which could have profound implications for European agriculture and organic farming. The Commission proposes introducing a single decoupled income payment per farm. This payment should be based on historical payments. 'Decoupled' means that the farm will receive the payments regardless of what it produces. Any payments are subject to compliance with specific environmental, animal welfare and food safety requirements (cross-compliance). A further element of the mid-term review with specific relevance to organic farming is the inclusion of a new food quality chapter in the rural development regulations, which should encourage 'farmers to participate in quality assurance and certification schemes recognised by the member state or the EU including geographical indications and designation of origin and organic farming' . In addition, the Commission suggested introducing support to producer groups for promotion activities

– and here too, organic farming is mentioned among other types of farming. The final important element of the mid-term review proposals is a quasi-mandatory farm audit which – according to the Commission – should help farmers to 'become aware of materiel flows and on-farm processes relating to environment, food safety, animal health and welfare, and occupational safety standards'. The Commission also proposes to introduce compulsory long-term set-aside (replacing rotational set-aside) regulation of arable land.

The general line of the Commission proposals, namely to decouple large parts of the payments within the so-called 'first pillar' of the CAP and to shift more money to the second pillar for the benefit of the rural development programmes, is a step in the right direction. It is evident that the decoupled payment per farm is only a transitional solution and would lead, in the long term, to the abolition of this payment, because it is hard to imagine that politicians would be able to sell such 'payments for doing nothing' to taxpayers. As a transitional policy element it makes sense, however, because it paves the way for gradual change and leaves time and scope for the farmer to adapt to a new policy environment. Furthermore, such decoupled payments are much more compatible with WTO requirements than the current policy. It can be expected, however, that in certain regions, especially in those where arable land is used with low fertilising intensity in conventional production, land use might drastically change: set-aside might become the most profitable land use in those areas.

With respect to cross-compliance, the Commission paper is not very clear whether this only refers to existing environmental regulations for agriculture or whether new and additional requirements will be introduced. Similarly, for the farm audit, it is not clear whether this only refers to guaranteeing that the minimum environmental compliance already required by law today will be retained. In fact, mandatory farm audits might have a negative indirect effect on organic farming. It is quite likely that the standards conventional farmers have to meet in order to be part of the auditing system are very close or identical to the legal minimum requirements. In spite of this, consumers might think that conventional agriculture has become more environmentally friendly and thus see less necessity to buy organic products. Whether such a hypothetical development would actually have a net positive effect on the environment and animal welfare is very questionable. On the other hand, it is obviously quite a positive development if existing quality management systems in organic farming can be improved with financial help from the European

Commission as seen under the proposal for the extended Rural Development Regulation.

The abolition of rotational set-aside might be welcome from the viewpoint of some nature conservationists. However, quite a number of organic farms use rotational set-aside as a means to increase soil fertility. Complete abolition of this type of set-aside is therefore a disadvantage for organic farming. It would be advantageous for organic farming were a free choice between the two types of set-aside to be introduced, if only for organic farms. The Commission sees the need to maintain a mandatory set-aside for farmers receiving subsidies. This, of course, is surprising, given that the main appeal of the idea of decoupling lies in an expected decrease of production quantities: if agricultural production decreases because payments are decoupled, why then would mandatory set-aside be needed?

An important element of the Commission's proposals is that it would become possible 'to offer animal welfare payments for efforts that go beyond the mandatory reference level'. If such a proposal were implemented, this would extend the scope of the agri-environmental programmes considerably. Depending on its practical implementation, this might lead to a significant increase of animal production systems with high priority given to animal welfare even in conventional agriculture. This might also impact on the market for organic products, possibly negatively influencing price levels.

At the time of writing this book (January 2003), it seems unlikely that major parts of the European Commission's proposals within the mid-term review will actually be adopted by the European Council. However, even if, in the short term, other political considerations may override fundamental agricultural reform, it seems likely that the Commission's ideas from the mid-term review will influence the discussion after the Agenda 2000 period has ended in 2007, when fundamental agricultural reform is likely in any case.

The future perspectives of organic farming within the framework of Agenda 2000 largely depend on the further recognition of its role in achieving the overall policy and agricultural objectives of environmental cross-compliance, rural employment, reduction of surpluses, food safety and other related welfare issues. There are signs that organic farming is receiving increasing attention in this respect, both in the European Commission and in some member states. For example, in May 2001 the Danish Agricultural Ministry, together with the European Commission, organised an international conference on 'Organic Food and Farming –

Towards Partnership and Action' in Copenhagen. Several European agricultural ministries and high-level officials participated, and agreed on the Copenhagen Declaration (see Box 4.1). In this Declaration, the European Council, the Commission and the European governments were called upon to pursue the process towards a European Action Plan for organic farming.

Box 4.1 **Declaration from the European Conference 'Organic Food and Farming – Towards Partnership and Action in Europe', 10-11 May 2001, Copenhagen, Denmark**
(Bjerregaard *et al.* 2001)

In signing this declaration from the European conference 'Organic Food and Farming — Towards Partnership and Action in Europe', 10-11 May 2001 in Copenhagen, Denmark, we wish to highlight that:

• Organic farming is a highly relevant tool, which contains the potential to participate in solving simultaneously a range of problems related to food production, environment, animal welfare, and rural development.

• Organic food and farming is becoming a major opportunity for food producers in Europe, due to a growing consumer interest in certified organic products. This is a precondition for developing a market for organic food and creating income for farmers.

• Organic food and farming should be developed further in Europe.

Experience from various countries in Europe demonstrates that the development of organic food and farming has been facilitated by Action Plans, i.e. strategic actions developed and undertaken in close partnership between the public and the private sector, including consumers, farmers, producers, retailers, non-governmental organisations (NGOs), researchers and other important stakeholders.

In order to facilitate partnerships and actions also at European level, the Conference calls upon the Council, the European Commission and European governments to ensure that the process towards a European Action Plan will continue.

Within the next two years the European Action Plan should:

• Analyse the barriers to and potential for further growth within production, processing, trade and consumption of organic products in Europe. ➡

➡

- Present a consensus-oriented and market-based strategy, which involves all stakeholders within Europe as a whole, including the European Commission, national governments, consumers, farmers, producers, retailers, NGOs, researchers and other important stakeholders.

- Cover all aspects concerning the development of organic food and farming in Europe, including areas such as environmental protection, animal welfare, consumer behaviour, market development, food safety, food quality, regulation, certification and labelling, research and international trade. By the choice of themes, the conference has itself covered all key aspects and thereby produced a range of specific recommendations which should be used as an input to the European Action Plan.

- Analyse the relationship between, on the one hand, the opportunities for the further development of organic food and farming and, on the other hand, the Common Agricultural Policy and other international agreements including WTO and Codex Alimentarius.

The declaration was signed by 17 European agricultural ministers and high-level officials.

The European Commission showed early reluctance to support such an action plan. Nevertheless, after some negotiations, the European Council on Agriculture released its own, toned-down declaration (Box 4.2). This was still positive about further support for organic farming, if it lacked some of the enthusiasm of the Copenhagen Declaration. After intensive discussions within the Commission and consultations with an external expert group, the Commission produced a working document on analysing 'the possibility of a European Action Plan for organic food and farming' (EC 2002a).

The Commission's working document includes a description of the development of organic farming as well as an attempt to analyse the current situation. It does not suggest a coherent set of actions but only recommends reflection on a number of broader issues connected to organic farming which could possibly become part of a European Action Plan (Box 4.3).

Among the major weaknesses of the working document is the lack of a strategic view of the role of organic farming within the context of agricultural policy. The Commission fails to answer the key question: what role it foresees for organic farming in comparison with other farming systems.

Box 4.2   Organic food and farming: European Council on Agriculture conclusion, 19 June 2001 (EC 2001)

The Council

- recognises organic farming as one way to achieve sustainable development;

- notes the importance of Council Regulation 2092/91 of 24 June 1991 on organic production of agricultural products and indications referring thereto on agricultural products and foodstuffs;

- notes that the member states, within the framework of their Rural Development Programmes, in accordance with Council Regulation 1257/1999 of 17 May 1999, have the possibility to promote organic farming;

- recognises the importance of the ongoing work regarding inter alia labelling of organic fodder, control of the organic production and implementing the rules on organic livestock;

- notes that the consumer interest in organic products increases in Europe;

- invites the member states, the Commission and stakeholders to share ideas on what further action at European Union level could facilitate production, processing, trade and consumption of organic products in Europe and, in the light of these ideas;

- invites the Commission to analyse the possibility of a European Union Action Plan to promote organic food and farming and present appropriate proposals.

The paper does not even include a clear statement about whether an Action Plan is desirable at all. Furthermore, it lacks in-depth analysis of the necessary revisions the CAP might have to undergo if organic farming is to be supported more strongly, and connections between a Plan and the mid-term review remain unclear. While reference is made to an expert group involved in the preparation of the paper, large parts of the advice given by members of that group have been ignored. For example, the expert group recommended abstaining from the mandatory use of the European organic farming logo. According to the minutes of the Council meeting, one of the few specific suggestions Commissioner Fischler made on the Action Plan was his support for compulsory use of this logo.

Box 4.3   **European Commission's view on possible elements for a future European Action Plan for organic food and farming** (EC 2002a)

(...) With a view to an Action Plan, further reflection could be carried out on the following issues:

- developing and facilitating various systems for organic produce sales;

- targeting organic farming to environmentally sensitive areas;

- encouraging the exchange of technical information between farmers;

- ensuring that the Common Agricultural Policy supports the development of organic farming;

- ensuring traceability and organic food authenticity.

Some actions can already be based on existing instruments such as information and promotion campaigns and rural development schemes... The major purpose of these actions would be the development of the market for organic produce. Another element acting upon enhancing consumer demand, but for which no legal instruments are required, could be to collect existing information and statistical data in order to carry out an agro-economic analysis of the organic market. The collected information and results of the analysis should be communicated to the various actors in the supply chain.

Other possible elements have been identified as deserving further reflection; they present advantages and disadvantages that should be raised in the discussion process to elaborate the European Action Plan. They relate mainly to the following subjects:

- the means to reinforce the use of the EU logo;

- access to information on additional inspection requirements where they exist;

- the harmonisation of testing methods, control procedures, supervision and accreditation, together with efficient cooperation between all actors involved in the inspection system, including Community inspections;

- the implementation of appropriate standardised procedures to ensure that imported products respect both fair competition with EU products and EU commitments regarding developing countries;

➡

- the establishment of a body for delivering independent, excellent and transparent advice on which production methods, substances etc. can be accepted in order to assure conformity with the principles of organic farming;

- the collection and communication of official statistical data on production, consumption, and trade (EU imports and exports) on a more permanent basis;

- the effective funding of research in organic farming from the point of view of food safety and quality, including expanding research into the development of new products and processing methods and the environmental sustainability of organic farming, and into comparison studies between organic and conventional food.

This is just a small example of the struggle at the political level. Nevertheless, it illustrates the development towards a more positive recognition of organic farming in European politics, despite opposition. A positive recognition in future CAP reforms and the general political climate are the most important factors defining the future of organic farming in Europe (Zanoli *et al.* 2000).

EU enlargement

Since the fall of the Berlin Wall in 1989, the idea of an enlarged European Union to include the Central and Eastern European countries has been envisaged by many policy makers and other actors. The original ideas for the integration and accession of the Central and Eastern European (CEE) countries have gained pace over the past ten years. Decisions were made at the European Council meeting in Copenhagen on 12 and 13 December 2002, when the Danish presidency stated: 'Today marks an unprecedented and historic milestone in completing this process with the conclusion of accession negotiations with Cyprus, the Czech Republic, Estonia, Hungary, Latvia, Lithuania, Poland, the Slovak Republic, Slovenia and Malta. The Union now looks forward to welcoming these states as members from 1 May 2004' (EC 2002c) (Figure 4.1). It was also stated that it was an EU objective to include Bulgaria and Romania as members in 2007. The decision whether accession negotiations will be taken up with

Figure 4.1 Countries being considered for EU accession
(Bichler and Schuster 2002)

Turkey was postponed until 2004 and was linked to a number of conditions.

The enlargement of the EU has both political and economic consequences. Politically, the idea of a 'greater' Europe has always been on the minds of supporters of European integration. It is, indeed, a unique and historic opportunity. The integration of a large part of the continent, extending a zone of stability and prosperity to new members, is an unprecedented opportunity.

Enlargement will also have a significant economic impact. The first and most obvious consequence will be the expansion of the single market from 370 to some 500 million consumers, together with an ample process of integration and the strengthening of the Union's position on the world market.

To achieve this, prior to accession, candidate and accession countries must undergo a process of further alignment with EU standards and adopt the EU body of legislation (*acquis communautaire*). Pre-accession criteria were therefore defined for both the private and public sector. In the words of the Commission (1997), 'economic and social cohesion will become even more important in an enlarged and therefore more diversified Union'. The pre-accession strategy involves strengthening the applicant countries' institutional and administrative capacity to apply the *acquis* while bringing their enterprises into line with the above-mentioned standards.

In macro-economic terms, the benefits of an enlarged Union are widely recognised:

- a single set of trade rules;
- a single tariff; and
- a single set of administrative procedures.

This will simplify dealings for third-country operators within Europe and improve conditions for investment and trade. At the same time, enlargement will allow higher mobility of human and financial resources, with potential welfare benefits for all European citizens.

On the other hand, the diversity of interests within the Union will increase. This may generate considerable pressure for sectoral and regional adjustments. Many of the pre-accession instruments are devised to tackle these potentially harmful effects of enlargement. They are designed to assure:

- macro-economic stabilisation;
- civil rights and other issues of democracy;
- harmonisation of legislation; and
- the gradual establishment of free-trade relations between the EU and the candidate countries.

Agricultural policy is one of the critical issues in accession negotiations. For the EU, application of the system of support to farmers in accession countries would have been very costly. After all, support had been designed to compensate for price reductions realised in 1992 and within the framework of Agenda 2000. In accession countries this would have had unwanted effects: support payments bound to cultivated land finally benefit the owners of the land, not necessarily the farmers.

Naturally, the accession countries also want benefit from the advantages of the EU system. If complete slaughterhouses must be retrofitted to European standards, some additional benefit must also be the result. It was decided in Copenhagen to phase in the EU's direct payments gradually, starting with 25 per cent in 2004 and eventually rising to 100 per cent in 2013. Several of the measures agreed were designed to take particular account of the large number of small farms and the existence of durable semi-subsistence farming, on the one hand, and the existence of a large-scale commercial farming sector on the other. In order to ease the transition for the semi-subsistence farms, a special measure of up to €1000 per year is offered. The idea behind this is to ensure that these structures, which also serve as a social safety net, are not destroyed during a phase of rural restructuring, in order to avoid growing rural unemployment and poverty.

Simplified systems for implementing direct payments allow decoupled payments for a transitional period if the administrative structures to manage the complicated EU system are not yet in place. This decoupled approach resembles elements of the European Commission's mid-term review proposals (EC 2002b). As in the existing EU, the new members will also benefit from rural development measures which could be financed by the EU up to 80 per cent. Relative to the budget of the first pillar of the CAP, the budget for rural development in the new member states will be higher than in the old member states.

The impact of enlargement on the organic farming sector is difficult to predict. The adoption of the EU body of legislation in accession countries will most likely result in some kind of support for organic farming under the agri-environmental programmes and possibly under other measures set out in the Rural Development Regulation. The existence of a wide spectrum of low-input farms in these countries might lead to a considerable number of farms opting for conversion: this may increase market pressure within the EU and dampen the interest of farmers in Western Europe in organic farming.

Those most exposed to price competition seem to be beef and dairy producers, as well as some fruit and vegetable producers. In these sectors, price is not the only competitive leverage. Certification and compliance with EU standards, traceability and residues are much more relevant for the organic market and the consumer. For example, in 2001 organic beef, fruit and vegetables were under-supplied in most EU countries, especially at the time of the BSE and Foot and Mouth Disease crises. Thus establishing certification systems and transport and processing networks is one of the challenging tasks of accession countries. Lower wages will probably ensure that these countries have a competitive advantage for years to come, especially for the production and processing of organic food.

In Western European countries, modernisation of farming during the last five decades has often meant highly intensive conventional farming. Only in a second phase, when the disadvantages of this type of modernisation became apparent on many farms, has conversion to organic farming taken place. Agriculture in the new member states is far less intensive and is also quite small-scale in many cases. This offers the opportunity for farmers converting to organic farming to bypass 'chemical modernisation' and to modernise their systems – which will also mean enlarging farm size – while going organic at the same time. This type of conversion from low-input systems that have traditional characteristics long forgotten in Western European agriculture poses very specific challenges to farmers, to advisory and research systems, and to governments. There are very few role models for this type of transition to organic farming. On the other hand, if farmers in the candidate countries who are already operating in the more commercially-oriented, large-scale sectors want to convert to organic farming, they will find many examples in the existing member states.

Summary

Organic farming is expected to develop rapidly in accession countries. Accession countries will export organic products. In the medium term, accession is a strong incentive to shift EU agricultural policy to the 'second pillar' of rural development and agri-environmental measures. Organic farming should benefit from this development. On the other hand, limited EU funds will be distributed differently. Accession countries will receive a high proportion of funds and less funds will be available for 'traditional' EU countries – even though a number of Western European politicians are still fighting this development. The expected expansion of organic farming in accession countries will most likely put pressure on prices for organic products – unless demand increases significantly.

WTO negotiations

Trade policy used to be a relatively narrow field of action, primarily of interest to exporting or importing businesses. Recently public awareness about the possible local and non-economic impacts has grown with international trade talks and agreements.

The World Trade Organisation provides the institutional and legal framework for multilateral trade. It came into being on 1 January 1995. The agreement which sets out its role, structure and powers is the first text in the package of Uruguay Round agreements signed in Marrakech on 15 April 1994. The Uruguay Round of the General Agreement on Tariffs and Trade (GATT) pledged to achieve a higher degree of trade liberalisation by committing all WTO members to converting all barriers to trade into tariffs and gradually reducing their tariff levels. This decreases support for agriculture and the amount of subsidised exports.

On certain issues, no agreement was reached in the Uruguay Round negotiations and a 'peace clause' was included in the Agreement: participants committed themselves to abstaining from retaliation in order to facilitate continuation of dialogue on unresolved matters. Presumably, the peace clause will end in 2003 unless an extension is negotiated.

In WTO terminology, subsidies in general are identified by 'boxes' which are given the colours of traffic lights: green (permitted), amber (to be reduced), red (forbidden) (Table 4.1). As usual, things are more complicated in agriculture. The Agriculture Agreement has no red box, but there is a blue box signifying exemptions for certain types of subsidies and for developing countries.

The blue box is an exemption from the general rule that all subsidies linked to production must be reduced or kept within defined minimal levels. It covers payments directly linked to acreage or animal numbers, but under schemes which also limit production by imposing quotas or requiring farmers to set aside part of their land. Countries using these subsidies say they distort trade less than alternative amber box subsidies. As matters stand, the blue box is a permanent provision of the Agreement. Some countries want it scrapped because the payments are only partly decoupled from production. Others say it is an important tool for supporting and reforming agriculture, and for achieving certain 'non-trade' objectives.

Green box domestic subsidies are also subject to discussion. Some countries would like to review the domestic subsidies listed in the green box because they could have an influence on production or prices under certain circumstances. The EU approach to the WTO conflict on the green box issue is that the specific role of agriculture as a provider of public goods should be recognised (EC 1999d). Measures that aim at protecting

Table 4.1   The WTO boxes: international trade agreements and agriculture (WTO 2001)

Amber box	All subsidies and other domestic support measures considered to distort production and trade. Their total value must be reduced. **Examples:** Market price support and input subsidies.
Green box	Subsidies that do not distort trade or cause minimal distortion. These subsidies are not subject to reduction commitments, but must be government-funded (not by charging consumers higher prices) and must not involve price support. **Examples:** Research, extension, food security stocks, disaster payments, 'decoupled' income support, and – currently – agri-environmental measures.
Blue box	Acceptable but temporary subsidies that should help to prepare further reforms over time. Exemptions from the general rule that all subsidies linked to production must be reduced or kept within defined minimal levels. **Examples:** Direct income payments ('partially decoupled'), market price support with production quotas (e.g., milk), headage and area payments

the environment should be accommodated in the Agriculture Agreement. The same applies to rural development measures and those aimed at promoting the sustainable vitality of rural areas and poverty alleviation. In particular, the Cairns Group of agricultural exporters (led by Australia, but including South Africa and most of the South American countries) would like a tighter definition of the green box. They argue that measures to encourage farmers to avoid environmentally damaging practices disregard the 'polluter pays' principle.

The issue can be summarised in terms of the measures allowed under the green box. Serious conflicts exist regarding the way in which the generally accepted principle of sustainability should be translated into agricultural policy. The EU and some other countries accept that agriculture is not only about producing food and fibre. They also consider other functions of agriculture: non-trade objectives such as ecological sustainability, food security, structural adjustment, rural development and poverty alleviation. In other words, there is a general agreement on the multifunctional role of agriculture.

Therefore in the WTO, two questions are debated:

- Are trade-distorting subsidies – or subsidies outside the green box – needed to help agriculture perform its multiple roles?

- Are all subsidies included in the 'green box' genuinely free from trade distortions, given that in some cases they can influence prices or production levels?

The most important aspect for organic farming is whether payments received through the agri-environmental programmes for environmental benefits remain in the green box. An increase in these payments for organic farming leads to an overall reduction in production. On the other hand, it also results in a higher production of certain products – organic products. If the concept of multifunctionality is taken seriously it should benefit organic farming by increasing recognition of the sector as an ecologically sustainable way of farming.

The term 'multifunctionality' may be abused occasionally in daily political life, but it remains a useful concept. Government intervention is not always a bad thing but is justified in some cases – even in cases where a distortion of trade results. The question, however, is which instruments to use to achieve this concept of multifunctionality.

The WTO negotiations will influence the future of European agriculture significantly. This will probably lead to a substantial reduction of market protection. Whether the EU will manage to conserve certain types of subsidies that recognise the multifunctionality of agriculture remains to be seen, but is unlikely.

As barriers to trade are further reduced, European agriculture depends increasingly on prices paid for agricultural products on world markets. In the past these were substantially lower than prices paid in the EU. Different prognoses on the development of world market prices exist – even optimistic forecasts. Assuming unchanged average prices, European agriculture will suffer income reductions unless the 'second pillar' of EU agricultural policy is extended. It remains to be seen if all measures that fall in the 'second pillar' today will be included in the green box.

This very broad view of the role of agriculture can be summarised as multifunctionality. For the EU the term also implies that subsidies and interventions in the agricultural sector are possible outside the green box to help agriculture fulfil its multiple roles. However, supporters of trade liberalisation argue that a fashionable term – no more – is being used by the EU to protect European agriculture from world competition.

The recognition in WTO negotiations of organic farming as a producer of valuable public goods could only increase recognition of the sector as an ecologically sustainable 'promised land' and would almost certainly lead to a large-scale uptake of organic farming in European agriculture (Zanoli *et al.* 2000). The importance of WTO renegotiations for organic farming has now been recognised, but lobbying by the organic movement started relatively late. Thus the interests of organic farming are in some danger of neglect, especially if the environmental benefits of organic farming are not quantified more precisely (Einarsson 2000).

Apart from the possible impact of the WTO agreements on levies, export subsidies and direct payments for agriculture, organic farming's economic viability substantially depends on how the market recognises the different quality of organic products. Labelling and certification schemes – already in place in the EU, and also applicable to imports (Lampkin and Midmore 2000) – are also expected to be accommodated in the WTO. In this context, two issues need to be discussed: the direct impact of labelling and certification, and the indirect impacts of GMOs.

The approval of the Codex Alimentarius Guidelines for Organic Food was an important step towards international harmonisation of government regulations. It acknowledges that organic farming standards are a legitimate means of recognising product quality rather than a technical barrier to trade. Therefore, policies that serve the development of organic farming undoubtedly fall into the current green box and are very likely to be treated as such in future negotiations. These Codex Guidelines are expected to gain increasing importance in relation to equivalence judgements on imported products under the WTO rules. Furthermore, they are expected to help build consumer trust. This becomes especially relevant for trade in organic food, as the designation 'GMO-free' is an important motivation for consumers to buy organic food.

In general, WTO negotiations often include GMOs under the heading of food safety. A simple labelling solution is discussed which would allow free trade of GM agricultural products – theoretically in order to satisfy consumers. This is a serious threat to organic farming. Cross-pollination and contamination of foodstuffs can reduce consumer confidence in organic products and raise production and certification costs for organic farmers (Bock *et al.* 2002).

In October 2002 the EU's new GMO Directive came into effect, under which new products require a full environmental risk assessment before any GM release, as well as full consultation with all interested parties and compulsory monitoring during the trials and post-release stages. Any licence will only be granted for an initial ten-year period. The new Directive replaces one that had been in force for the previous ten years but, as long as traceability, labelling and liability remain unaddressed, the moratorium on the introduction of new GM products in the EU remains in place. Individual member states must still approve the legislation, and France, Italy, Denmark, Austria, Greece and Luxembourg have made it clear that they want the labelling and traceability laws to be in place before they lift the moratorium.

The new EU Directive was the subject of a dispute that occurred in early 2002, especially with the United States. According to official spokesmen, the US was ready to launch a trade war over European plans to label all GM food. The European Commission considers that it has now fulfilled its commitment to create conditions for restarting the authorisation procedure for GMOs (thus avoiding being sued by the US under WTO rules). Companies must now decide what products they want to put on the market, and member states are responsible for initiating the authorisation procedure.

At the same time, the EU was ready to lodge a complaint with the WTO against the new US Farm Bill, which would substantially increase subsidies to US farmers. At the WTO ministerial meeting in Doha in November 2001, the US exerted great pressure on the EU to agree to modify or cancel its system of farming export subsidies, but the Farm Bill of 2002 appears to conflict very strongly with what was agreed in Doha. The Bill has also contributed to a breach in the historical alliance between the US and Canada on trade issues; Canada's government has strongly opposed the new US legislation and the relationship between the two countries has been deteriorating steadily.

The further development of WTO negotiations and their impact on organic farming seem even harder to predict than the effects of EU enlargement. While some critics claim that organic farming is a protectionist system *per se*, we see the possibility of WTO negotiations developing in a direction that would also benefit organic farming. Obviously, negative scenarios are also possible, a possibility highlighted in the next chapter.

Possible futures

The external policy developments that seem likely to influence organic farming most decisively in the future were discussed in previous sections.

Undoubtedly, EU policy developments as well as WTO negotiations will be important factors influencing the future of organic farming. Other relevant factors are listed in Table 4.2.

An attempt to analyse the influence of these factors on the organic farming sector can be made with the scenario technique, an integrative tool often used by businesses, government agencies and scientists to limit the range of possible futures. The aim is to understand what could happen under certain circumstances rather than to predict the future.

A scenario analysis for the organic farming sector in the European Union was conducted by an international group of scientists (Zanoli *et al.* 2000). Three of the resulting scenarios for the year 2000 are presented in the following boxes (Boxes 4.4–4.6). The aim is to provide a lively picture of each of the different scenarios within which organic farming might have to operate in the future. For illustration these scenarios are presented in the words of three hypothetical subjects:

Agronews Broadcast, a radio station specialised in agricultural issues;

John Dairy, who gives us the average farmer's opinion; and

Mrs Maggie Pie, a consumer.

The results of the scenario analysis are presented in Figure 4.2 for further illustration. Although only three possible scenarios were described here (Organic paradise, Surprise-free/Business as usual, Gloomy liberalisation), this helps readers to understand the purpose of a scenario analysis. What can be learned from this exercise? Is it not very confusing to confront so many different possible futures? One important message to keep in mind for the final chapter of this book is that the future is inherently uncertain. Any policy decision will always assume that certain conditions will persist and others will change. It is important to understand some of the factors governing future policy developments. Thinking through different scenarios helps to foster an understanding of the situation.

The scenario analysis concluded that the most influential and crucial determinants of future development in organic farming are:

1 the agricultural and agro-environmental policy which will come into effect after the implementation of Agenda 2000;

2 the Millennium Round of WTO negotiations;

3 the future perceptions and attitudes of consumers and society towards issues concerning food safety and the use of modern biotechnology in food production (Zanoli *et al.* 2000: 54).

Meanwhile, we believe that EU enlargement has to be added to this list, an issue that has been raised earlier in this chapter.

The values and perceptions of consumers and citizens are the key to the future development of organic farming. We believe that this can only be partly translated by market forces into economic and social reality. The reasons and justifications for policy interventions were discussed in Chapter 3. The next and final chapter addresses the question of how to approach and implement this intervention.

Table 4.2   Factors determining the future of organic farming and organic farming policy (Zanoli et al. 2000)

Food scares	The level of perception in society as a whole of all issues concerning dangers to food safety such as BSE, salmonella, etc.
Consumer confidence	Consumer confidence in economic prosperity, both in terms of the economic situation and consumers' socio-logical characteristics (social status, home location, etc.) and their interrelationship.
Farmers' altruistic concerns	All environmental and ethical issues as perceived by producers.
Controversial techno-logical changes in conventional farming	Process and product innovations stemming from agricultural and biological research which are controversial to farmers and to society as a whole; only highly controversial innovations such as biotech, GMOs, etc.
Market globalisation	All issues of market globalisation including the political ones: WTO, EU enlargement, impact of US Deparment of Agriculture (USDA) organic standards and Codex Alimentarius on EU regulations, etc.
CAP reform	All changes to be made to EU agricultural and food policy, i.e., Agenda 2000 and Council Regulation 2092/91 reform.
Consumer price of conventional products	Prices for conventional food products paid by final consumers in the market.
Farm-gate price of conventional products	Prices for conventional products obtained by farmers.

Box 4.4   Gloomy liberalisation (Zanoli et al. 2000)

The purpose of this scenario is to describe the impact of deregulation and globalisation on organic farming, where the EU experiences a deep economic crisis and a generally austere economic environment.

Agronews Broadcast: We are experiencing a reduction in trade barriers for agricultural commodities which is increasing competition among farmers. Among other things, this is due to the strong development of innovations relating to products and processes in agriculture. This situation creates increasing operational difficulties for farmers, who in some cases can be forced out of the market.

The news is bad on the demand side as well: consumer confidence is low, while concerns about the impact of food quality on health are increasing, given the difficulty and confusion surrounding the identification and traceability of foodstuffs.

The current approach to agricultural and trade policy is leading to a substantial reduction in farming support, accompanied by a general price reduction in agricultural commodities resulting from growing global competition. Organic farmers cannot escape the negative trend in agricultural commodities, and their only chance of maintaining a market share depends on their ability to adopt marketing strategies that can justify a price premium for organic products. The negative situation for the general agricultural environment is reinforced by farmers' greater propensity to focus on economic aspects rather than on environmentally friendly agricultural practices, which become less important as farmers face severe economic difficulties.

Mr J. Dairy: I am quite worried about the strong reduction in policy support for agriculture, and I wonder how farmers can face the abolition of subsidies: competition with non-EU countries is growing rapidly, and I am afraid that many of my colleagues may not be able to cope with the low prices without some financial support. It is really hard to imagine adopting different/new agro-environmental practices, especially as the EU does not give support any more. Anyway, even if I wanted to do it all by myself, I don't think I could: it's difficult to find somebody to give me advice or training on how to adopt organic farming techniques, and there are very few technical innovations for organic farming. Consumers also have their own problems dealing with the downturn in the economy, and do not seem very interested in the more expensive organic products.

Mrs M. Pie agrees: Under these circumstances, I'm afraid I can't worry

➡

too much about the quality of the food I eat. In fact, I see lots of consumers who are worried that their income will be reduced in the near future, and others who are no longer sure of keeping their jobs because of increasing competition and economic instability. Anyway, environmental issues seem to have been forgotten: nobody talks about them any more, the media rarely focus on the environment or organic farming, and politicians are usually more involved in solving other social and economic problems. Who knows, maybe the environment and food quality are not major issues anymore.... And even if I wanted to buy organic food, it's getting difficult to find it in the shops, as it is not well advertised, and there is not much choice, as the range of organic products is quite poor.

Mr J. Dairy: The reason for the poor availability of organic products depends a lot on the low demand for them: you know, only rich households can afford to eat organic. Prices are actually quite a bit higher than conventional products, not only because of the difficulties of farming organically, but also because of the high processing and distribution costs involved. At the end of the day, the farmer gets a very low price for organic products, but the consumer has to pay much more. Believe me, it would not be very convenient for me and my colleagues to farm organically, which is why you cannot expect a great variety of organic products. Why don't you try some of those intermediate standard products? It seems that those who produce them can take advantage of the confusion and the poor control on organic products, and sell them as organic, and I doubt you'd be able to tell the difference....

Box 4.5   Surprise-free scenario (business as usual)
(Zanoli *et al.* 2000)

This scenario describes the development of the organic sector in the context of the EU's Agenda 2000. The general policy attitude towards organic farming is slightly positive. The organic sector is mainly supported through the application of the Rural Development Regulation (Council Regulation 1257/99).

Agronews Broadcast: The underlying assumption of policy makers seems to be that European agriculture needs to increase its competitiveness in order to face international competition without as many flanking measures. The globalisation of the agricultural markets is increasing as a result of the lowering of barriers to free trade: the result is a fall in farm-gate prices which is only partially transferred to consumer prices.

Farmers see this situation as being potentially negative for their income, and their main concern is to maintain as much of their competitiveness as possible, even if this means sacrificing environmental issues. No changes are envisaged in social attitudes towards food safety or the goals pursued by farmers

Increasing globalisation leads to reduced consumer confidence in economic and social welfare, but the public is also extremely worried about the long-term effects of genetically modified food products and about other controversial technological changes in agriculture.

Mr J. Dairy: Well, things have not changed a lot over recent years, and from where I'm standing, farmers have the same problems as ever. Prices are now much lower, because of the gradual reduction in EU support, and there is growing competition from products coming from other countries. In this situation, organic farming cannot help, I'm afraid. I can see that there could be some potential demand for organic products, and some CAP measures can still be of help for organic farming, but I don't think it's enough. In fact, the situation in the organic sector is quite depressing: there are no product or process innovations in organic farming that might stimulate improvements in production techniques or raise the quality of organic products over that of conventional ones. This situation implies that there is an almost total absence of research, information and training for organic farmers. Besides, farm-gate prices are much lower than those paid by consumers, because the marketing sector is still underdeveloped, and the agro-food industry seems to have little interest in processing organic products. Maybe it is because they do not believe in the positive evolution of the sector.

Mrs M. Pie: I would buy some organic food, because I really do not like all those strange genetically modified products coming from heaven knows where, but the problem is that their prices are quite a bit higher than other products, and, you know, nowadays money is an issue! It seems that only rich people have the right to eat good food…. Anyway, I have to say that even if I had more money, organic food would not be as appealing as it should be, because there are so few products to choose from, and they are not advertised at all: sometimes it is difficult to identify them or to distinguish them from other products.

Mr J. Dairy: Mrs Pie, you are right I think this is due to the lack of information on labelling and certification for organic products: it is difficult enough to farm organically and, at the end of the day, if you cannot sell your products as organic, well, it's nonsense if we don't even get any extra money. Under these conditions, organic farming is not a good option: after all, we farm to make a living, not to take care of the environment!

Mrs M. Pie: Well, given all these difficulties with organic products, I might try some of those from integrated agriculture: they look just as good as the organic ones, and are probably better than the GM ones.

Box 4.6   Organic paradise (Zanoli et al. 2000)

This scenario depicts the conditions that are considered optimal – though realistic – for the development of organic farming in Europe. Two variants have been considered, one with a low degree of market liberalisation and higher price levels for agricultural commodities, and the other with slightly higher market liberalisation, and lower price levels. Results have shown negligible differences between the two versions, if we exclude intermediate standards and, to a lesser extent, organic product prices.

Agronews Broadcast: Europe is experiencing a period of prosperity and economic stability which has increased consumer welfare and confidence. Consumer expectations of economic growth are higher, and they are therefore likely to consume more. With a higher standard of living, consumers are more interested in quality of life, and this generates greater interest in quality food products and environmental issues.

The concept of quality assumes a broader significance. It now concerns not only the nutritional and health-related aspects of the products, but also their ability to meet and satisfy consumers' needs. Food safety increases, and so does consumers' confidence in what they eat. Worries about genetically modified products and other controversial technological changes are prompting more consumers to buy organic products, which they view as safe and guaranteed.

Farmers are taking an increasingly active role in the debate on the ethical, cultural and environmental implications of production processes. Maximising profits is no longer their only objective; instead, it is accompanied by numerous other goals, including protecting the environment.

Mr J. Dairy: I am pleased to see that all the conditions to stimulate the supply of organic products are in place: more research, better information and technical advice, and technological innovations, and I am proud to say that this positive situation has largely developed thanks to the significant involvement of farmers in changing the shape of the agricultural business in Europe. Farmers can now be considered to be playing an active role in the environment. But it would be unfair not to acknowledge the great support of the EU institutions and the essential role played by the consumers. Actually, these three elements have jointly worked to produce what it is no exaggeration to describe as a 'paradise' for organic farming. CAP has given a great deal of support to agro-environmental measures, with a specific focus on organic farming. A great many measures have been proposed, not only financial — like direct income subsidies or marketing development measures — but also operational, and many activities which exert a positive impact on the environment, such as agro-tourism and rural development, have been encouraged. Consumers have also shown such an interest in organic products that even farmers who have long been sceptical about organic farming have decided to convert.

Mrs M. Pie: You know Mr Dairy, I really do not see any reason why I should not buy organic products: their quality has increased a lot recently, and now the product range is really large. There are a lot of good advertisements for organic products, and labelling has also improved, so that now it is easy to find them and distinguish them from conventional products. By the way, I have to say that I do not really like all the new technologies they are using for ordinary food products: I do not think they are either ethical or healthy. I know that conventional products are a little cheaper than organic ones, but money is not the only thing in life!

Mr J. Dairy: Well, conventional products are cheaper, but organic products are not expensive anyway: now that supply has increased so much, prices have dropped. Nevertheless, organic farming is certainly a good bargain, and I would say that it is much more profitable than conventional farming, because of the high demand and EU support. Also, it is much easier to sell organic products to the processing industry or to distribution channels, as farmers have now achieved a good stable production level, while the processing and marketing sectors have greatly improved their capacity to deal with organic products.

I notice that the greater attention being paid to environmental issues and health has also benefited products from integrated agriculture; these have more or less maintained their market share, despite the success of organic products, and the only losers seem to be the conventional producers. Organic farming is indeed the most efficient and innovative way of farming!

Mrs M. Pie: Do you think that the positive situation for organic products could be maintained even if the EU adopted a more liberal trade policy?

Mr J. Dairy: Yes, I think so, although at the moment, trade barriers have been substantially reduced compared to a few years ago, so things would not change a lot. Simply, I would expect prices to drop a little, also for organic products, but this will be a further advantage for you consumers. The only major change I can imagine is that under these conditions, farmers producing intermediate standard products may experience some difficulty: consumers who really care about environment and health now have a wide range of organic products at reasonable prices, while the others feel protected by the overall improvement in the hygiene and safety of foodstuffs in Europe.

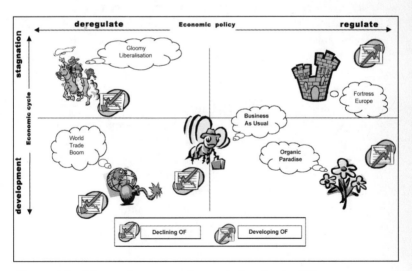

Figure 4.2   The performance of organic farming in different scenarios in Europe (Zanoli *et al.* 2000)

CHAPTER 5

Recommendations for future organic farming policy

What should politicians make of the picture we have presented in this book? This final chapter is intended to answer that question and give some indication of how to proceed. Of course, any decision on political action has to be based on a thorough analysis of the situation, as described in the overview of organic farming in Europe today in Chapter 2.

It should also take into account the contributions organic farming can make to policy objectives, as discussed in Chapter 3, as well as theoretical aspects of agricultural policy. A changing policy environment offers opportunities for, but also poses threats to, the development of the agricultural sector in Europe and, of course, the development of organic farming.

If the readers of this book were convinced that organic farming does not deserve any public policy support, there would be little point in trying to define the best support policy approach. However, for readers who believe that – in line with one or more of the arguments presented in Chapter 3 – organic farming deserves public intervention, the question which arises is what kind of intervention is appropriate. As a starting point, it is useful to remember that policy makers are just one of several groups of actors in the subsector of organic farming, which means that while public policy may have an influence, it often cannot control the outcome of policy implementation: other actors involved might react in unforeseen ways, and there may be external forces far beyond the agricultural sector that may also exert considerable impact on organic farming.

An integrated approach

We strongly recommend following an integrated approach to organic farming policy. Action plans have been shown to be a useful means to pursue this. They can avoid the pitfalls of contradictory policies, they offer the opportunity for broad stakeholder involvement in the shaping of policy, and their development can provide a forum for establishing a vision and a plan for policy action on organic farming. Most importantly, action plans require a clear and long-term commitment by policy makers to co-ordinated organic farming policies.

Policies relevant to organic farming have not always been coordinated effectively on a European level. The same holds true for policies within a number of member states. Different elements of organic farming policy are operated independently without any recognition that in practice they are all connected. The most obvious example of such developments is that policy makers responsible for determining the level of subsidies for organic farming within the agri-environmental programmes often do not feel responsible for market developments in organic farming. If subsidies for organic farming increase while all other factors remain constant, it is likely that prices for organic products will fall and organic farmers might actually be worse off than before. It is therefore essential that these linkages between supply and demand are considered when policies are devised.

Another example concerns the scale of subsidies for organic farming compared to integrated farming. In some cases, there is practically no difference between the two, so it is not surprising that under such schemes farmers would rather use integrated practices, which are far less restrictive than organic farming although they bring fewer environmental benefits.

Many promising measures that are potentially very helpful for the further development of organic farming have not been used at all or only on a very small scale up to now. Examples include the provision of frequently updated information on the organic market – still scarce throughout the European Union – or support for technology development. It would make sense to have a systematic plan that addresses these areas: this could be beneficial to further development without too much financial involvement by governments.

The development of such an action plan can itself be viewed as a catalytic process where networks between actors within the organic subsector are formed. These actors are not only policy makers within administrations, parliaments and governments, but also include many others: consumers, farmers and everyone involved in the processing, distribution and marketing chain for organic products. A discussion process that might be initiated by the government but includes all these stakeholders could also foster cooperative, non-governmental solutions and closer collaboration within the sector.

Several countries have already implemented action plans for organic farming. For example, Denmark introduced its first action plan for organic farming in 1995. This resulted in an intensive discussion among all stakeholders in the agricultural sector and gave a strong impulse to the development of the organic farming sector. In 2001 Germany's new Minister of Agriculture initiated a national programme for organic farming focusing on the provision of information. In future, this programme will be part of a national action plan for organic farming. Intensive discussion and a hearing of all interest groups in the organic sector resulted in a document outlining a programme supporting the development of the organic farming sector in Germany (Bundesprogramm Ökologischer Landbau) (Isermeyer *et al.* 2001). The document was drafted by a small group of scientists and stakeholders at the Minister's request.

As European policies are the dominant factor in the agricultural sector and the European level is gaining importance in the marketing of organic products, it makes sense to develop organic farming policies on a European level, rather than merely at national and regional levels.

While the scope and content of political action plans vary widely, any coherent plan must address the following issues, which will be used here as a structure for discussion:

- analysis of the present situation, and the identification of barriers and potentials;
- objectives and strategic decisions;
- instruments and addressees;
- priorities;
- follow-up, monitoring and control.

Status quo analysis

A thorough review of the present situation is a key element of any action plan. Differences in opinion on the best combination of instruments are often rooted not only in different objectives but also in varying assessments of the starting conditions. A first step in any action plan is to produce a coherent description of the situation at the outset. In the following sections, we offer a short summary of views we presented earlier in the book. We concentrate on the barriers that a European action plan must overcome. However, the opportunities will also be examined and appropriate instruments discussed.

The following barriers impede the further expansion of organic farming within the current 15 EU member states:

1 Organic products in most member states are difficult to identify, even for consumers who are sympathetic and interested in them.

2 Overall, the organic sector is too small to benefit from economies of scale, especially in the chain between farm gate and point of sale to consumers, which leads to comparatively high costs. These in turn necessitate high premium prices and are one reason why only a relatively small number of products is available in supermarkets. These factors deter the potential 'new organic consumer' from actually buying the products. With low levels of demand, the situation stays unchanged. (Interestingly, there are examples from member states where this does not apply to certain products; for the majority of member states, however, it seems to be correct.)

3 Council Regulation No. 2092/91 and subsequent legislative provisions have much improved the certification system. However, consumer confidence in the certification and control system could be enhanced.

4 Demand for foodstuffs can react very flexibly within a matter of days, while the supply of agricultural products is more inflexible because of the long timescales required in any production process. The flexibility of response of organic supply is even lower than that of a conventional farming system because of the required transition period.

5 For most farmers, the transition to organic farming is a long-term strategic decision which usually implies a planning horizon of a decade or more. Only with confidence that markets and policy will be favourable to organic products over an extended period is it feasible to convert to organic farming. This is especially true if the high costs of transition for certain types of farms are considered: in animal husbandry, high investments are often needed in order to comply with organic standards.

6 While Agenda 2000 is slightly more favourable to organic farming than the previous EU policy package, the general measures contained in the Common Agricultural Policy are often not conducive to organic farming.

7   It is difficult to get reliable and up-to-date information on the organic sector. This includes market and policy information, as well as technical information needed by farmers.

8   Some of the biological–technical problems affecting organic farming have not been adequately resolved by research. For other problems solutions exist, but distribution of this information to farmers is sometimes poor.

9   There is a great deal of insecurity surrounding the further development of European agricultural policy, and this must be taken into account. In particular, the compatibility of specific support measures for organic farming with WTO criteria and negotiation outcomes must be considered. EU enlargement is likely to limit the political opportunities to provide larger-scale financial support for organic farming. On the other hand, the enlargement of the EU offers potential for wider adoption in those countries. Some of the low-input and small-scale agriculture existing in the Central and Eastern European countries could possibly 'go organic' directly, thus avoiding the 'detour' of intensification followed by conversion to organic farming that has been typical in many of the Western European countries.

10 International trade issues are a threat to organic farming in some instances as well. If the 'peace clause' and green box measures are called into question in the future, the comparative political advantage enjoyed by organic farming will disappear. The issue of free trade in respect of GMOs and GM products also poses a potential threat to European organic farmers, because they would not be able to guarantee that organic products are GMO-free.

This list of issues – while by no means exhaustive – gives an impression of the conditions which must be considered by politicians dealing with organic farming.

Objectives and strategic decisions

A number of strategic decisions have to be made in any attempt to develop a coherent plan for organic farming support. Often, these strategic decisions are not discussed openly, but are simply implied in the policies themselves. These strategic decisions closely relate to the action plan's objectives. Clarity on these objectives – combined with a well-founded analysis of the situation at the outset – is a necessary prerequisite when devising an effective package of policy measures.

We thus argue clearly that governments should work with stakeholders in the agricultural sector to develop a vision for organic farming. This vision could be modest ('organic farming as a niche market') or ambitious ('20 per cent of farming to be organic in 2010'). Such a vision could see organic farming primarily as an environmental instrument or as a market opportunity, or base support on maintaining the viability of a techno-logical option outside a GMO-oriented and chemically intensive agriculture ('organic farming as insurance if the development of conventional farming leads to a dead end'). The vision should develop a position on the regional implications of organic farming and could be protectionist or non-protectionist. To us, it seems highly desirable that politicians should clearly discuss their objectives and strategic decisions as a foundation for specific policy measures.

The weight given to organic farming and alternatives

Some member states of the EU have set targets for organic farming and in so doing have given a clear answer to that question. The most recent and probably most ambitious target was set by the German government, which is seeking to increase organic farming area and even market share to 20 per cent within the next ten years. The Copenhagen Conference on organic farming, organised by the Danish government and discussed in the previous chapter, concluded that it is desirable to have a European organic farming action plan that would set quantitative targets (see Box 4.1, p. 98).

These developments are only the most recent in a much longer chain of events in which Denmark, Austria, Sweden and Switzerland have led the field for a number of years and which show an increasing awareness among politicians of the potential of organic farming. In our view, the question of how much priority should be attached to organic farming is a political decision. In order to make a balanced judgement it is necessary take other options into account as well. For example, organic farming is not the only way to produce environmental benefits through agriculture. If the intention is to achieve a broad spectrum of environmental objectives, organic farming seems to be a good instrument. To reach very specific objectives, targeted agri-environmental measures within conventional farming or alongside organic farming might be more cost-effective (Stolze et al. 2000).

Reasons to support organic farming

Two major lines of argument exist: organic farming can either be supported because it produces public goods and helps to achieve policy objectives like animal welfare (Häring *et al.* 2001), or it can be seen as a market opportunity, 'an organic market to conquer' (Kalden 2001). It is, of course, also possible to combine both views. The importance given to either view has major implications for policy development.

If the market is stressed and the public good issues are neglected, any direct subsidisation of farmers which is not geared to overcoming periodic obstacles in farm organisation or marketing planning will not be part of the political programme. On the other hand, if the public goods produced by organic farming and its advantages over competing agri-environmental options are considered on their own merits, measures aimed at increasing transparency and overcoming the structural problems within the organic sector seem irrelevant.

We believe that both arguments are true: organic farming is a market with considerable development potential, but it also produces public goods, and it seems reasonable to support it so that it can continue to do so. As the market is still small and lacks critical mass (the logistical costs between farm gate and final outlet are often too high), and as farmers need a certain level of confidence in order to convert, it makes sense to provide a medium-term political commitment to give more support to organic farming by direct subsidies on the ground that public goods results. These subsidies would help to create a viable organic market by providing farmers with mid-term confidence in the profitability of conversion to organic farming, thus encouraging more farmers to convert. At the same time, the potential market will develop as a result of increased transparency. If demand also rises as a consequence of this greater market transparency, the market might increase in size to a point where economies of scale in the logistical chain reduce price premiums on organic products.

The spatial strategy

Is organic farming predominantly a system for disadvantaged and less favoured regions, where it is often found today? Public intervention in favour of organic farming usually aims at increasing the land area under organic farming management. However, this objective should be qualified in spatial and temporal terms. We learned in Chapter 2 that organic farming is unevenly distributed throughout the European regions. Marginal regions are over-represented, while the most fertile regions exhibit a very low percentage of organic farming acreage. If organic farming is to be integrated into agricultural policy, there are two possible strategies. One would be to increase further the concentration of organic farming in the less fertile regions. These marginal areas are often of great interest in terms of nature conservation objectives, and organic farming seems to be a useful element in development strategies for disadvantaged and less favoured regions as it produces a broad range of environmental advantages.

The other strategy is a more even application of organic farming methods across regions and farm types, based on the argument that the greatest benefit from the introduction of organic farming in a given area is gained where conventional farming is carried out intensively. Supporters of this view also argue that a division of the European landscape into nature conservation areas, where organic farming is used in a substantial part of the area and where environmental goods and services are important, and fertile areas, where there is little concern for the environment, is the wrong strategy.

Protectionist vs non-protectionist support for organic farming

Politicians serve their constituents. This is the fundamental wisdom of modern politics. If we apply this to the organic farming sector, it seems logical that politicians are likely to show certain protectionist tendencies in their responses to organic farming. A protectionist policy would inhibit imports for colleagues from third countries. However, when public goods are produced and paid for by the public through their taxes, this is not protectionism. On the other hand, there seem to be a number of indications that protectionist tendencies do exist in the organic farming sector. Sometimes these are expressed in a shift away from the common European standard, usually to a stricter standard. If processers adhere to this stricter standard, it may be very difficult for organic products produced to meet the lower European standard to maintain their market position. Sometimes, too, state-supported logos or labels assert a regional or national preference. Such strategies are not always successful. The national German logo ÖPZ, which was launched in 1999, has been a failure. One of the reasons given by the sector is that the logo was heavily biased towards German products. If a German organic product was available, the processer was not allowed to use foreign organic products if he wanted to use the logo. A similar example concerns the European logo for organic food, which is not awarded to products produced outside the EU.

We argue that it is important to have regional products and to label them as such. However, this should be done in addition to the labelling of organic products, not included in the organic label. We are strongly in favour of a non-protectionist approach, as this has a number of advantages. Most importantly, the general idea of the Council Regulation (see p. 123 above) on organic products was to allow free trade within the EU; counter-vailing policies conflict with the general principles enshrined in this Regu-lation. Furthermore, a single non-protectionist logo or labelling approach has the potential to increase the organic market substantially – more than if market development is hampered by protectionist policies. In sum, non-protectionist organic policies may even be beneficial to those who were initially in favour of protectionism. However, as there is a strong reliance in organic philosophy on local and regional resources and regional con-sumption, additional acknowledgement of the products that are genuinely of regional or national origin might be useful; this could be achieved by combining other labels or logos with the organic one.

Instruments and addressees

A more or less coherent plan for the further development of organic farming should consider five areas of action:

1 informing the consumer, especially by developing a unified approach to a widely recognised common logo based on Council Regulation 2092/91 and subsequent legislation;

2 improving the functioning of the organic chain: production, processing, distribution within the supply chain – with major emphasis on improving information, education, technology development, research and extension support;

3 financial support to organic farmers as remuneration for the production of public goods;

4 reviewing related policies with direct influence on organic farming, such as the general development of common agricultural policies, tax laws, etcetera (the objective is to identify measures that negatively influence organic farming and change these);

5 supporting cooperation between conventional and organic farmers' organisations in the institutional environment and, as far as possible, building a consensus on the long-term objectives of organic farming.

While the first three of these measures have clear groups of addressees, – consumers, actors in the processing chain and producers – the other two fields of action are of a more cross-sectional nature. They refer to all the groups, and possibly beyond.

Informing the consumer

Demand for organic food is probably the single most important variable for the future of organic farming. In the current situation, actual demand for organic food does not fully realise its potential for a number of reasons. The crucial obstacle to the full realisation of potential demand is lack of transparency in the market from the viewpoint of the consumer. In most countries, consumers encounter a variety of labels. This is very confusing and also impedes free trade between the countries of the EU.

If the organic market is to continue to grow, consumers must be able to distinguish easily between organic products and conventional products. Having taken over the defining power from the organic farming movement, the responsibility here lies with European policy. The existence of the European logo for organic farming is an acknowledgement of this responsibility. However, in its current version, the European logo is not very well-suited to the task in hand.

Nonetheless, the argument put forward here for a new single European logo for organic products should not be understood as a substitute for attempts to develop the regional character of organic foodstuffs more strongly. There are a number of initiatives in this area and there are many opportunities to support them under the new rural development rules. It is important to see these two approaches as complementary rather than mutually exclusive. Until now, a European-wide approach to market transparency – a need consistently highlighted in this book – has been notably and completely absent.

European labelling is unlikely to succeed in the market without a major campaign to raise consumer awareness of the label or logo. Such a campaign might be less expensive than campaigns which attempt to establish other brands, products or labels in the market, because many consumers already have a generally positive attitude to organic products. The campaign would promote the interests of the organic farming sector as a whole. However, it may not suit the interests of many of the individual actors within this sector, as establishing the European logo in the marketplace devalues other logos to some extent, even if these logos continue to exist alongside the European logo. Farmers' associations and other label owners may therefore oppose this move as their investment in their own labels may lose value.

Despite this possible opposition, there is a strong case for a European campaign to establish a European logo. First, organic farming is a classic case of a sector producing positive external effects. If the sector could be expanded by realising potential consumer demand, this would be a very desirable situation because public goods would be paid for by consumers as a by-product of private goods. A further advantage of a marketing campaign to establish a new European organic farming label is that it only needs a major effort in the first year, with minor efforts (recall marketing) in subsequent years. This is quite different from the situation in other areas of public support where continuous commitment is necessary.

However, in order to ensure the success of the marketing campaign, it is necessary to review the approach that resulted in the adoption of the European logo for organic farming. A successful logo must clearly distinguish organic from other products. Moreover, all organic products must be able to use that logo; indeed, for consumers, it would be desirable to find that logo on all organic farming products. It is useful, then, to regard a logo as supporting organic farming in general, not just within Europe. Naturally, this notion does not conform with the view that European organic farmers would be the only beneficiaries of a new European organic farming logo. However, there are two arguments to be considered here. One is that the EU's organic farming regulations have been very influential and in some respects have actually come close to being the world standard for organic farming. With influence, of course, comes responsibility.

The other argument refers to the fact that many imported organic products create synergies in realising the potential demand for organic products, as availability of many specialist foods is still a problem. The availability of a wider product range might also benefit products produced in the European Union. It could thus be argued that if potential demand is actually realised by a much more transparent system for the consumer, there might be a net benefit for European organic producers if increased market transparency leads to a total market expansion. Drawing from the experiences of some member countries, it is vital that use of the European logo is free for producers. The possibility of mandatory use could also be considered, as this might be desirable from the consumer's point of view.

Once a new European logo is developed along these lines, it is imperative to introduce it into the market and publicise it quite quickly. In order to achieve the desired results, substantial sums of money are necessary for a first-wave marketing campaign. It is important to assess the amounts needed for such a campaign in relation to the sums spent on supply-side subsidies for organic farmers via the agri-environmental programmes. These supply-side subsidies are currently estimated at €600 million per year in the EU. If a quarter of that figure were budgeted for a one-off campaign, amounting to €150 million per year, and a tenth for recall campaigns in subsequent years, it is likely that the desired effect could be achieved.

Of course, any information campaign has to be developed with and carried out by professional agencies experienced in that field. Moreover, it must be European but still tailored to the needs of the individual countries. This is quite a demanding task. Market turnover of organic foods in the EU is currently estimated at €7 billion per year (ITC 1999). The objective of such a campaign would probably be to double market demand within three years. The expected increase in turnover also puts the demands on the marketing budget into perspective.

Such an approach would be new within the European context. However, if European policy decides that organic farming should be an important part of European agriculture in future, marketing the idea of organic farming through a new organic farming logo seems to be an effective way of making use of money that is intended for organic farming support. In the light of this fact, this new policy step may be necessary and justified.

Improving the functioning of the organic chain

The logistical chain in organic farming is currently not working efficiently in every respect. The links in the chain are the inputs bought by organic farmers, especially those which are specific to the sector, such as organic seed, the production process on the farms themselves, and especially the further distribution, processing and marketing beyond the farm gate up to the point of sale to the consumers. Focusing on this chain as a whole is very important for two reasons. First, consumer confidence that products are genuinely organic relies on the smooth operation of every part of the chain. It is therefore very important to ensure that reliable, transparent and similar standards exist in all member states and regions with respect to the certification and control process. The inspection reports issued by the European Commission following its review of the certification systems in certain countries make it clear that there is further room for improvement in the working of this chain. This is also be very important in easing trade within the EU. Any suspicion that the certification system in another region might not be as strict as in the producer's own region might induce implicit (or even explicit) protectionist measures.

Another important issue within the supply chain is information. The situation regarding the reliability of information in the organic sector is very unsatisfactory, as a recent example (Kuhnert *et al.* 2001) illustrates. In February 2001 the new German Minister of Agriculture, Renate Künast, set a target of 20 per cent market share of organic products by 2010 in Germany. In order to assess whether such a target is realistic or not, it is essential to determine market share at the outset. However, no government statistics existed on this figure. The estimates provided by scientists, private companies and other interested groups varied considerably. For instance, an article in the renowned *Lebensmittelzeitung* put the share of total turnover of organic food products in Germany at 2–3 per cent, whereas the organic market expert Ulrich Hamm estimated it to be a little over 1 per cent. Information on total market share of organic products is not important only for policy makers: everyone involved has an interest in the size of the market. As Kuhnert *et al.* (2001) point out, calculating market share on the basis of the number of farms in a given area is by no means a straightforward task. Imports and exports are intervening factors, the production structure of organic farming is quite different from conventional farming, and there are no reliable data on the number of animals and the share of certain crops, to say nothing of quantities harvested or the amount of milk and meat sold. Moreover, some products are not sold as organic but enter the conventional market, often because distribution networks are lacking, especially in the case of milk. On the other hand, prices of organic products are higher than those of conventional products but seem to vary considerably (Michelsen *et al.* 1999; Hamm *et al.* 2002). Taking all these factors together, it is clear that without a serious effort to improve the information base, political measures will be operating on extremely shaky ground. The lack of up-to-date and reliable price information in the market is especially serious, despite efforts by a number of member states.

However, it is not only market information that is scarce. If significant numbers of farmers are to convert, they will need to learn new techniques. While the basic agricultural practices are identical in conventional and organic farming, much of the thinking and many of the more detailed aspects are not. Providing farmers with easy access to information is therefore an important part of any policy to develop the organic sector. This holds especially true of practical training at all relevant levels in the agricultural sector, from farmers' practical training up to universities. Any growth scenario for organic farming has to take account of the fact that education and training take a considerable length of time.

It is not simply a matter of compiling existing information and making it available to the people who need it. For a strong increase in organic farming, new information and, above all, new technologies are required. In the conventional sector, it is increasingly recognised that at least parts of technological progress and research can be financed privately by the producers of seeds, pesticides and fertilisers. By contrast, organic farming is based on the fundamental idea that the use of these inputs in production should be greatly reduced; instead, they should be replaced by intelligent measures and specific technologies which draw to a far greater extent on the farm's own resources. Organic farming is not opposed, *per se*, to modern technologies; it simply advocates a very careful selection of the technologies to be used. Some of the information technologies available may have specific potential for organic farming in order to monitor closely the processes on the farm. The adaptation and development of these technologies cannot be expected to a significant degree from a private sector selling inputs to the farmer. For this reason, there is strong justification for government intervention, as well as a need to steer research organisations much more actively into the area of organic farming.

Financial support to organic farmers

The current political framework allows direct payments specifically to organic farming. These direct payments vary widely between member states and regions in the member states. They reflect the argument that organic farming provides public goods such as environmental benefits. However, from the perspective of the organic food market, any direct subsidisation is critical.

Although there may be some justification for this type of support, based on the public goods argument, the current support system must be carefully reviewed in order to keep a level playing field between different regions and member states in Europe.

Typically, the payments are granted on a per hectare scale, both to converting and continuing organic farmers. Limiting payments to converting farmers is a hazardous process, as conversion might be undertaken simply to secure the payments, with reconversion after the eligibility has ended. Furthermore, the justification of producing public goods is also lost. Investment initiatives with a preference for organic farming – support for the construction of animal pens which conform with animal welfare and organic standards, for example – can be a sensible means of temporary assistance.

With respect to the scale of the subsidies paid, the following should be considered: for the decision to convert, the long-term reliability of any policy in favour of organic farming is much more important than short-term gains. The decision to convert is a long-term strategic decision for the farm. Thus, attractive support programmes are necessary. A differentiation of payments between farm types and regions might be justified under certain conditions, just as today intensive organic vegetable producers often receive higher payments than producers of extensive beef.

Reviewing related policies

No organic farming policy functions in a vacuum. Organic farmers and the organic sector are part of a regulatory framework which often influences the sector in a haphazard way. It is therefore important to examine such policies more closely. For instance, European agricultural policy must be reviewed in detail in order to determine whether it can be adapted in any way in order to promote organic farming. One example is the decision to allow organic farmers to grow legumes for fodder on set-aside areas. This provision – introduced into the CAP in 2001 – gives much more flexibility to organic farmers' crop rotation, and in many cases actually allows subsidies that previously were unavailable to be paid to organic farmers for fodder production. Even without any major change in agricultural policy, it is helpful to examine policy details in order to identify areas where such improvements are possible.

On a more general note, it is quite likely that European agricultural policy will undergo some measure of reform around the time of the mid-term review in 2003, and most certainly in 2007 when the Agenda 2000 planning period ends. If politicians pursue the objective of increasing the extent of organic farming, policies that redesign financial support for agriculture on lines that reduce reliance on production quantities will promote organic farming. For example, financial support for beef production is still coupled to the number of animals reared and produced. As organic farming has a less intensive system and fewer animals per hectare, it generally profits less.

A similar argument applies in relation to other agri-environmental measures that might incorporate a financial advantage to organic farming in order to reflect its actual environmental benefits. While such benefits are very difficult to quantify in monetary terms, it is obvious that they go far beyond those delivered by integrated approaches, and this should be reflected in the subsidies paid.

Other areas, beyond the subsidy system operated within the CAP, could also be examined. One option, for example, is to offer special tax breaks for organic farming. For instance, there is a proposal that organic farming could be supported by lowering VAT on organic products compared with conventional products. This would make organic products cheaper and be of direct benefit to consumers. For political reasons, it may be difficult to take this step at present, and there are obviously a number of legal obstacles at European level. However, this is essentially an example of a negative eco-tax on organic food products. On the other hand, state intervention in other parts of the food market can also influence the organic food market and therefore have a considerable (negative) impact on the organic sector. For example, if governments introduce a state-supported logo for integrated farming, this might add to consumers' confusion, prompting them to buy the integrated products in the mistaken belief that they are organic. Until now, efforts to promote the widespread adoption of integrated logos and trademarks have not been very successful; indeed, most of the initiatives – even when launched with considerable public relations support – have withered away. Governments should therefore be aware of the potential negative effects of such initiatives on the organic sector.

Supporting cooperation in the institutional environment

A last major point concerns actions which relate not to financial measures and regulations but to the 'soft' institutional context in which organic farming operates. There is evidence that organic farming benefits from being 'in conflict' with the conventional sector while cooperating with it at the same time (Michelsen *et al.* 2001). On the one hand, a certain degree of confrontation is necessary in order to ensure that the organic sector maintains its clear profile and distinct identity. On the other hand, cooperation which gives organic farming access to much of the institutional framework established by the conventional sector can be a significant boost to the development of organic farming.

This approach relates primarily to relations between the two sectors. It is an approach which is relevant to most of the actors within the sector, not only to politicians. However, broad consensus among stakeholders and political parties on a medium- to long-term commitment to the development of organic farming is a major positive factor. If this is a credible commitment for businesses, farmers, marketing agents and others involved in the sector, it makes sense for them to invest in organic farming. Creating this consensus and building stakeholder confidence is a major risk-reducing factor. A further advantage is that it is not directly related to any specific government expenditure but simply creates a positive environment. It is clear – as is borne out by experiences with the Danish action plan – that even the process of devising such an action plan and accepting it as a policy measure builds confidence in future development.

Priority instruments

We are strongly in favour of a balanced action plan that includes a variety of elements. However, in the past, direct support to farmers has been relatively overrated in organic farming policy. We think there is a case for substantially increasing total support to organic farming; however, the first priority should be to give relatively more weight to policies which aim to provide information to the European consumer. Thus the proposals relating to the adoption of the European organic food logo deserve the highest priority in a European Action Plan which contains a range of different instruments.

Monitoring and control

It may seem premature to think about the monitoring and control of the European Action Plan at this stage. However, if such a plan is devised and implemented, continuous monitoring of developments within the sector on a European scale is essential. Up-to-date information must be available in order to identify potential problems which might reflect weaknesses in the plan. This monitoring, and reactions to it, could have institutional implications: it is by no means certain whether the European institutions would be equipped to deal with this task, or whether reorganisation is necessary. This should be an issue for review.

Conclusions

What has been presented here, of course, is not a detailed action plan but merely the potential framework for an action plan. In order to bring this process to a successful conclusion, it is important to involve the stake-holders in a systematic way. Consumers, organic farmers, conventional farmers, the health food sector, supermarket chains, different levels of administration and scientists should be brought together in a politically led process in order to formulate an action plan.

One option would be to commission a small group of representatives of different stakeholders to develop an action plan for organic farming in Europe. This approach is likely to be much more promising than leaving the task to government agencies, which has tended to be the method adopted in the past. However, it can only be successful if certain pre-requisites are met: there must be active backing and continuous feedback from high-level politicians across member states and at EU level, and professional support as well as support from experts, technical staff, ministries and other public organisations. This group approach would allow the positive experiences gained in individual member states (such as Denmark and Germany) to be utilised to the full.

Box 5.1   Key recommendations

There are five key policy areas for the further development of organic farming in Europe.

Informing the consumer
A key aim is developing a unified approach to a widely recognised common logo, possibly based on European Regulation 2092/91 and subsequent legislation.

Market transparency does not exist in many cases at the moment, and thus the potential of consumers to support organic farming is not fully exploited. The objective should be to foster the development of domestic markets, especially in CEE countries, in order to avoid a complete reliance on exports.

Developing a clear policy on genetically modified organisms and making it clear to consumers what can, and cannot, be the role of organic farming in this context.

Improving the functioning of the organic chain
The focus here is on production, processing and distribution within the supply chain, with major emphasis on improving information, education, technology development, research and extension for organic farming and its process chain.

➡

The aim is to enhance technical and financial performance and the delivery of public goods through targeted research and information dissemination. The current lack of statistical information and general analyses of the functioning of the organic market is a very important issue.

The regulatory system needs further development. Specifically the system of import authorisations to the EU should be further developed and all countries should aim to establish systems that are fully compatible, transparent and easy to administer. Accreditation systems could play a key role in achieving this objective, with the potential for fruitful involvement by non-government actors like IFOAM.

Another need is to develop comprehensive information on the situation in the Council of Europe member states: standards, policies, production, trade and consumption statistics. The amount of money currently available for research in organic farming does not correspond to the envisaged importance of organic farming and the processing of organic products.

Supporting organic farmers financially as remuneration for the production of public goods

Specifically, within agri-environmental programmes and rural development policies, organic farming should be supported in accordance with its potential to achieve a broad range of environmental and other objectives. Organic farming should receive a financial advantage over other approaches in this area, in relation to its actual environmental benefits. While these are very difficult to quantify in monetary terms, it is obvious that they go far beyond any offered by integrated approaches, and this should be reflected in the premiums paid.

Prioritising organic farming

Supporting advisory services for organic farmers and producers as the preferred management approach in specific regions may be as important as direct payments.

Reviewing related policies

Policies with direct influence on organic farming – such as the general development of common agricultural policies, tax laws, etcetera – need to be reviewed. No organic farming policy functions in a vacuum: organic farmers and their sector are part of an institutional and regulatory setting which inadvertently influences organic farming, often by accident. It is therefore important to examine such policies more closely. For instance, the European agricultural policy must be reviewed in detail in order to see whether there can be adaptations that help organic farming.

The potential for tax credits and other means to support organic farming should be examined (examples include a pesticides tax, organic investment tax credits and reduced VAT for organic food).

Supporting creative conflict
Conflict between conventional and organic farmers can be a creative process that helps to build a consensus on the long-term objectives for organic farming.

Human capacity building and infrastructure development should be encouraged.

The establishment of trust between actors within the organic sector should be supported.

Finally, resources for sector development need to be targeted at actors with a long-term involvement and commitment.

It is important that policies for organic farming take the dynamic nature of the sector into account and make sure that there is a balanced application of supply/push and demand/pull measures by combining the key areas mentioned above in a manner adapted to the specific circumstances. In order to facilitate this it is recommended that member states develop action plans for organic farming which will then require periodic revision. It would be desirable if the EU could support the development of such action plans in the candidate countries.

References

Alrøe, H. K., E. S. Kristensen and N. Halberg (1998). 'A Systems Approach to Sustainability and Organic Farming'. Paper presented at the European Workshop on Research Methodologies in Organic Farming, Frick, Switzerland, 30 September–3 October 1998.

Alvensleben, von R. (1998). 'Nachhaltiger Konsum: Konzepte, Probleme und Strategien'. Special Supplement, *Agra-Europe*, 28 December 1998: 1–7.

Bichler, B. and H. Schuster (2002). Unpublished maps. University of Hohenheim, Stuttgart.

Bjerregaard, R., E. Argyris, M. Bötsch, N. Daver, P. Gæmelke, M. Gardfjell, H. Hanssen, K. Hemilä, C. J. Kalden, M. Kiklerius, R. Künast, G. Kuneman, W. Molterer, E. Morley, I. Padar, G. Rundgren and M. Winberg (2001). *Organic Food and Farming – Towards Partnership and Action in Europe.* Proceedings of the European Conference on Organic Food and Farming, 10–11 May 2001, Copenhagen, Denmark, p. 6.

Bock, A.-K., K. Lheureux, M. Libeuas-Dulos, H. Nilsgard and E. Rodriguez-Cerezo (2002). *Scenarios for Co-existence of Genetically Modified, Conventional and Organic Crops in European Agriculture.* Seville: IPTS–JRC, European Commission.

CAC (Codex Alimentarius Commission) (2001). 'Guidelines for the Production, Processing, Labelling and Marketing of Organically Produced Foods', CAC/GL 32. 1999; Rev 1 - 2001. Available from the Internet: <http://www.fao.org/organicag/frame2-e.htm.> 12 December 2001.

Compagnoni, A., R. Pinton and R. Zanoli (2001). 'Organic Farming in Italy'. Available from the Internet: <http://www.organic-europe.net/country_reports/italy/default.asp.> 7 December 2001.

Dabbert, S. (2000). 'Organic Farming and the Common Agricultural Policy: a European Perspective'. In Alföldi, T., W. Lockeretz and U. Niggli (eds.), Proceedings of the 13th International IFOAM Scientific Conference, pp. 611–14.

Dabbert, S. and J. Braun (1993). 'Auswirkungen des EG-Extensivierungsprogramme auf die Umstellung auf ökologischen Landbau in Baden-Württemberg'. *Agrarwirtschaft*, 42, 2: 90–9.

Dabbert, S., A. Häring, M. Stolze and A. Piorr (2000). 'Agrarpolitische Bewertung der Umwelteffekte des ökologischen Landbaus'. *Schriften der Gesellschaft für Wirtschafts- und Sozialwissenschaften des Landbaues* e.V., Vol. 36: 93–100.

Darby, M. and E. Karny (1973). 'Free Competition and the Optimal Amount of Fraud'.

Journal of Law and Economics, 16: 67–88.

DARCOF (Danish Research Centre for Organic Farming) (2001). 'The Danish Research Centre for Organic Farming'. Available from the Internet: <http://www.foejo.dk/GB/sider/darcof/index_darcof.html.> 7 December 2001.

Dewes, T. (1994). 'Der Wissenschaftsbegriff im ökologischen Landbau – Zur Konzeption ökologischer Landbausysteme'. In Mayer *et al.* (1994), *Ökologischer Landbau – Perspektive für die Zukunft*, Stiftung Ökologie und Landbau, Occasional Publication No. 58, pp. 16–27.

Dienel, W. (2000). 'Organisationsprobleme im Ökomarketing – eine transaktionskosten-theoretische Analyse im Absatzkanal konventioneller Lebensmittel'. Dissertation, Humboldt Universität zu Berlin.

EC (1991). 'Council Regulation (EEC) No. 2092/91 of 24 June 1991 on Organic Production of Agricultural Products and Indications Referring thereto on Agricultural Products and Foodstuffs'. *Official Journal of the European Communities*, L198 (22 July 1991): 1 15.

EC (1992). 'Council Regulation (EEC) No. 2078/92 of 30 June 1992 on Agricultural Production Methods Compatible with the Requirements of the Protection of the Environment and the Maintenance of the Countryside'. *Official Journal of the European Communities*, L215 (30 July 1992): 85–90.

EC (1999a). 'Council Regulation (EC) No. 1804/1999 of 19 July 1999 supplementing Regulation (EEC) No. 2092/91 on Organic Production of Agricultural Products and Indications Referring thereto on Agricultural Products and Foodstuffs to Include Livestock Production'. *Official Journal of the European Union*, L 222 (24 August 1999): 1–28.

EC (1999b). 'Agenda 2000 – for a Stronger and Wider Union'. COM (97) 2000 def. Office for Official Publications of the European Communities, Brussels. Available from the Internet: http://europa.eu.int/comm/agenda2000/overview/en/agenda.htm.> 12 December 2001.

EC (1999c). 'Council Regulation (EC) No. 1257/99 of 17 May 1999 on Support for Rural Development from the European Agricultural Guidance and Guarantee Fund (EAGGF) and Amending and Repealing Certain Regulations'. *Official Journal*, L 160, 26 June 1999: 80 – 101.

EC (1999d). 'EU Activities with the World Trade Organisation. Report to the European Parliament'. Working document of the Commission Services, Brussels.

EC (2000a). 'Agenda 2000 Budget – Financial Framework 2000–2006'. Available from the Internet: <http://europa.eu.int/comm/budget/en/cadrefinancier/cadrefin2000-2006.htm#03 > 15 April 2001.

EC (2000b). *Organic Farming. A Handbook to EU Legislation*. Brussels, 2000.

EC (2001). '2360th Council Meeting – Agriculture'. Press release, Luxembourg, 16 June 2001, Press: 241 – No. 9930/01. Available from the Internet: <http://ue.eu.int/newsroom/.> 6 December 2001.

EC (2002a). 'Analysis of the Possibility of a European Action Plan for Organic Food and Farming'. Commission staff working document, Brussels, December 2002.

EC (2002b). 'Communication from the Commission to the Council and the European Parliament: Mid-Term Review of the Common Agricultural Policy' COM (2002) 394 final, Brussels, July 2002.

EC (2002c). 'European Council: Presidency Conclusions Copenhagen European Council 12 and 13 December 2002'. Available from the Internet: <http://europa.eu.int/council/off/conclu/index.htm> 2 January 2002

EFRC (Elm Farm Research Centre) (1996). 'Research Priorities in Organic Farming in the UK', in-house publication.

EFRC (2001). 'Who We Are'. Available from the Internet: <http://www.efrc.com> 7 December 2001.

Einarsson, P. (2000). 'Agricultural Trade Policy – As If Food Security and Ecological Sustainability Mattered. Review and Analysis of Alternative Proposals for the Renegotiation of the WTO Agreement on Agriculture'. Stockholm: Forum Syd.

Eurostat (1999). *Eurostat Jahrbuch 98/99 – Europa im Blick der Statistik*. Fourth edition. Luxembourg: Amt für amtliche Veröffentlichungen der Europäischen Gemeinschaften.

Eurostat (2002). *Data on Organic Farming*. Eurofarm Databank.

FAO (2002). *Organic Agriculture, Environment and Food Security*. Environment and Natural Resources, 4. Rome: Food and Agriculture Organisation, 2002.

FAZ (Frankfurter Allgemeine Zeitung) 2001. 'Die jetzt angestrebte Agrarpolitik ist verfehlt'. 17 January 2001.

Fibiger Nørfeldt, T. (2001). 'Organic Agriculture in Denmark'. Available from the Internet: <http://www.organic-europe.net/country_reports/denmark/default.asp.> 14 August 2001.

Folli, A. and T. Nasolini (1995). 'Ricérca e sperimentazione sull'agricoltura sosteníbile in Italia'. *Annuàrio 1995*, Cesena: Osservatòrio Agroambienale.

FiBL (Forschungsinstitut für biologischen Landbau) (2003). FiBL-Portrait. Available at: <http://www.fibl.ch/english/fibl/portrait.php> 25 January 2003.

Foster, C. and N. Lampkin (1999). 'Organic and In-Conversion Land Area, Holdings, Livestock and Crop Production in Europe'. Technical Deliverable Report 2c. EU project Fair3-CT96-1794.

Foster, C. and N. Lampkin (2000). 'European Organic Production Statistics, 1993–98'. In *Organic Farming in Europe: Economics and Policy*, Vol. 9. Stuttgart-Hohenheim: University of Hohenheim.

Gerber, A. (2001). 'Vom Reduktionismus zur Transdisziplinarität: Leitbilder für eine zukunftsweisende Forschung im Ökologischen Landbau'. In H.-J. Reents (2001), Proceedings of (Sixth) Wissenschaftstagung zum Ökologischen Landbau: Von Leit-Bildern zu Leit-Linien, Berlin: Verlag Dr. Köster, pp. 31–4.

Hamm, U. and J. Michelsen (1996). 'Organic Agriculture in a Market Economy. Perspectives from Germany and Denmark'. In Troels Østergaard (ed.), *Fundamentals of Organic Agriculture*, Proceedings of the 11th IFOAM Scientific Conference, Copenhagen.

Hamm, U., F. Gronefeld and D. Halpin (2002). *Analysis of the European Market for Organic Food*. Aberystwyth: University of Wales.

Hansen, S. and T. Ruissen (1999). 'Thoughts on Research Approaches within Organic Farming'. In *Research Methodologies in Organic Farming*, FAO/REU Technical Series No. 58.

Häring, A. (2001). 'Impact Assessment of Different Policy Options on Organic Farming: Farm Level Case Studies'. EU-Project FAIR3-CT96-1794: Organic farming and the CAP. Technical Deliverable Rix.

Häring, A. and S. Dabbert (2002). 'Research on Organic Food Production: Status, Requirements and Perspectives'. In Zervas, G. and I. Kyriazakis, *Organic Meat and Milk from Ruminants*, European Society for Animal Production (ESAP) Publication No. 106, Wageningen: Wageningen Academic Publishers.

Häring, A., S. Dabbert, F. Offermann and H. Nieberg (2001). 'Benefits of Organic farming for Society'. Proceedings of the European Conference on Organic Food and Farming, 10–11 May 2001, Copenhagen, Denmark, pp. 80–8.

Hartnagel, S. (1998). *Statistik der biologischen Landwirtschaftsbetriebe in der Schweiz, 1997*. Frick/Basel: Forschungsinstitut für biologischen Landbau.

HDRA (Henry Doubleday Research Association) (2001). 'What is the HDRA?' Available from the Internet: <http://www.hdra.org.uk/about.htm.> 7 December 2001.

Henrichsmeyer, W. and H. P. Witzke (1994). *Agrarpolitik* Vol. 2, *Bewertung und Willensbildung*. Stuttgart: Verlag Eugen Ulmer.

Höök, K. (1996). *Ecological Agriculture and Horticulture: Research in Seven European Countries*. Stockholm: Swedish Council for Forestry and Agricultural Research. Available from the Internet: <http://www.wto.org/english/tratop_e/agric_e/ag_intro03_domestic.htm#conceptual.> 7 December 2001.

Hueth, B. (2002). 'Pesticide Use and Regulation: Theoretical and Institutional Considerations'. In Kuhl, M., P. M. Schmitz and S. Wiegand (eds.), *Cost-Benefits Analysis of Crop Protection*, Kiel: Wissenschaftverlag Vauk, pp. 30–5.

IFOAM (International Federation of Organic Agriculture Movements) (1996). *Basic Standards for Organic Agriculture and Processing and Guidelines for Coffee, Cocoa and Tea, Evaluation of Inputs*. Tholey-Theley, Germany: International Federation of Organic Agriculture Movements.

IOAS (International Organic Accreditation Service) (1999). *Annual Report 1999 of the IOAS*. Available from the Internet: <http://www.ifoam.org/accredit/ann_report99.html.> 18 August 2001.

IOAS (2001). 'Accreditation Update'. Newsletter No. 201, May 2001. Available from the Internet: <http://www.ifoam.org/accredit/news0501final.pdf.> 14 August 2001.

Isermeyer, F., H. Nieberg, S. Dabbert, J. Heß, T. Dosch and F. Prinz zu Löwenstein (2001). *Bundesprogramm Ökologischer Landbau – Entwurf der vom BMVEL beauftragten Projektgruppe*.

ITC (International Trade Centre) (1999). *Organic Food and Beverages: World Supply and Major European Markets*. Genf: International Trade Centre.

ITC (2001). 'Overview World Market for Organic Food and Beverages (2000 estimates)'. Available from the Internet: <http://www.intracen.org/itc/mds/sectors/organic/welcome.htm.> 14 August 2001.

Kalden, C. (2001). 'An Organic Market to Conquer – Experiences with a Pull-Oriented National Action Plan'. Proceedings of the European Conference on Organic Food and Farming, Copenhagen, 10–11 May 2001, pp. 168–71.

Källander, I. (2001). 'Organic Agriculture in Sweden'. Available from the Internet: <http://www.organic-europe.net/country_reports/sweden/default.asp.> 14 August 2001.

Keatinge, R. and I. Rasmussen (1999). 'Application of a Holistic Interdisciplinary Approach to Laboratory and Field Experiments'. In *Research Methodologies in Organic Farming*, FAO/REU Technical Series No. 58, Rome: FAO, pp. 123–5.

Keatinge, R., B. Cormack, S. Padel and M. Wolfe (2000). 'A Review of Current European Research on Organic Farming'. MAFF-Project OFO171. Available from the Internet: <http://www.adas.co.uk/organic/.> 10 August 2001.

Kingdon, J. (1995). *Agendas, Alternatives, and Public Policies*. New York: Longman.

Kirchmann, H. and G. Thorvaldsson (2000). 'Challenging Targets for Future Agriculture'. *European Journal of Agronomy*, 12: 145–61.

Kolbe, H. and F. Rikabi (2000). 'Studie zum Versuchswesen im Ökologischen Landbau in der Bundesrepublik Deutschland'. *Schriftenreihe der Sächsischen Landesanstalt für Landwirtschaft*, 5, 3: 1–48.

Kortbech-Olesen, R. (2002). 'Market Situation'. In Willer, H. and M Yussefi, *Organic Agriculture Worldwide 2002. Statistics and Future Prospects*, Stiftung Ökologie und Landbau (SÖL) Special Issue, 74: 29–35.

Kuhl, M., P. M. Schmitz and S. Wiegand (eds.) (2001). *Cost-Benefit Analysis of Crop Protection*. Kiel: Wissenschaftverlag Vauk.

Kuhnert, H., S. Wragge, P. H. Feindt and V. Beusmann (2001). '20% Ökologischer Landbau – Zielformulierungen, Maßnahmenvorschläge und Einschätzungen von Akteuren'. Available from the Internet: <http://www.soel.de/inhalte/ARCHIV/kuhnert_2001_01.pdf.> 7 May 2001.

Lampkin, N. (2001). 'Certified and Policy-Supported Organic and In-Conversion Land Area in Europe, 1985–2001'. Personal communication, 15 November 2001.

Lampkin, N. (2002). 'Certified and Policy-Supported Organic and In-Conversion Land Area in Europe, 1985–2001'. Available from the Internet: http://www.organic.aber.ac.uk /statistics/euroarea.htm. 4 December 2002.

Lampkin, N. and P. Midmore (2000). 'Opportunities and Threats for Future Policy Development: Agenda 2000 and the WTO'. Paper presented at the 13th IFOAM Scientific Conference, Basel, August 2000, mimeo.

Lampkin, N., C. Foster, S. Padel and P. Midmore (1999a). 'The Policy and Regulatory Environment for Organic Farming in Europe'. In *Organic Farming in Europe: Economics and Policy*, Vol. 1, Stuttgart-Hohenheim: University of Hohenheim.

Lampkin, N., C. Foster and S. Padel (1999b). 'The Policy and Regulatory Environment for Organic Farming in Europe: Country Reports'. In *Organic Farming in Europe: Economics and Policy*, Vol. 2, Stuttgart-Hohenheim: University of Hohenheim.

Latacz-Lohmann, U., G. Recke and H. Wolff (2001). 'Die Wettbewerbsfähigkeit des ökologischen Landbaus: Eine Analyse mit dem Konzept der Pfadabhängigkeit'. *Agrarwirtschaft*, 50, 7: 433–8.

Lindenthal, T., C. Vogl and J. Hess (1996). 'Forschung im Ökologischen Landbau – Integrale Schwerpunktthemen und Methodikkritiken'. *Förderungsdienst*, Special Issue, 2c.

Makatouni, A. (2001). 'What Motivates Consumers to buy Organic Food in the UK? Results from a Qualitative Study'. In Proceedings of the 72nd EAAE Seminar, Chania, Crete, June 2001, forthcoming.

Marchesini, L. (1992). 'La relazione domanda-prezzo eni prodotti dell'agricoltúra ecologica'. *Rivista di Economía Agrària*, 1, Bologna.

Michelsen, J., U. Hamm, E. Wynen, and E. Roth (1999). 'The European Market for Organic Products: Growth and Development'. In *Organic Farming in Europe: Economics and Policy*, Vol. 7, Stuttgart-Hohenheim: University of Hohenheim.

Michelsen, J., K. Lynggaard, S. Padel, and C. Foster (2001). 'Organic Farming Development and Agricultural Institutions in Europe: a Study of Six Countries'. In *Organic Farming in Europe: Economics and Policy*, Vol. 9, Stuttgart-Hohenheim: University of Hohenheim.

Mövius, R., A. Häring and M. Stolze (1998). 'Regional Distribution of Bioland Farms in

Germany – Unpublished Maps'. Stuttgart-Hohenheim: University of Hohenheim.

Müller, M. and U. Hamm (2001). *Verbrauchereinstellungen beim Einkauf von Lebensmitteln in Mecklenburg-Vorpommern*, Neubrandenburg: Schriftenreihe der Fachhochschule Neubrandenburg, Series A, Vol. 14.

Nelson, P. (1970). 'Information and Consumer Behaviour'. *Journal of Political Economy*, 78: 311–29.

Nieberg, H., F. Offermann and S. Padel (2001). 'Kein Patentrezept für die Ausweitung des ökologischen Landbaus'. In *Europa-Nachrichten*, Special Supplement, *Agra-Europe* 14, 1, 2 April 2001.

Niggli, U. (1998). 'Holistic Approaches in Organic Farming Research and Development: a General Overview'. In *Research Methodologies in Organic Farming*, FAO/REU Technical Series No. 58, Rome: FAO, pp. 33–9.

Niggli, U. (1999). 'Research in Organic Farming in Europe – Priorities and Needs'. In Proceedings of the Conference on Organic Farming in the European Union – Perspectives for the 21st Century, Baden/Vienna, Austria, 27–28 May 1999, pp. 177–81.

Niggli, U. and W. Lockeretz (1996). 'Development of Research in Organic Agriculture'. In Oestergaard (ed.), *Fundamentals of Organic Agriculture*, Proceedings of the 11th IFOAM Scientific Conference, Copenhagen, pp. 9–23.

Offermann, F. (2000). 'Quantitative Sector Modelling of Organic Farming'. Technical deliverable Rx of Project Fair 3-1996-1794, Braunschweig, Germany, unpublished, 48 pp.

Offermann, F. and H. Nieberg (2000). 'Economic Performance of Organic Farms in Europe'. In *Organic Farming in Europe: Economics and Policy*, Vol. 5, Stuttgart-Hohenheim: University of Hohenheim.

Olson, M. (1965). *The Logic of Collective Action*. Cambridge: Harvard University Press, 1965, p. 14.

Oskam, A. (1997). 'The Economics of Pesticides: an Overview of the Issues'. In Oskam, A.J. and R. A. N. Vijftigschild (eds.), *Workshop on Pesticides, Wageningen, 24–27 August 1995, Proceedings and Discussions*, Wageningen, pp. 360–84.

Osterburg, B., J. Wilhelm and H. Nieberg (1997). 'Darstellung und Analyse der regionalen Inanspruchnahme von Agarumweltmaßnahmen gemäß Verordnung (EWG) 2078/92 in Deutschland'. Braunschweig: Bundesforschungsanstalt für Landwirtschaft, Institut für Betriebswirtschaft, Arbeitsbereicht 8/97.

Padel, S. and J. Michelsen (2001). 'Institutionelle Rahmenbedingungen für eine deutliche Ausdehnung des ökologischen Landbaus – Erfahrungen aus drei europäischen Ländern'. *Agrarwirtschaft*, 50, 7: 395–9.

Pinton, R., A. Compagnoni and R. Zanoli (2001). 'Organic Farming in Italy'. Available from the Internet: <http://www.organic-europe.net/country_ reports/italy/default.asp.> 7 December 2001.

Pretty, J. N., C. Brett, D. Gee, R. E. Hine, C. F. Mason, J. I. L. Morison, H. Raven, M. D. Rayments and G. van der Bijl (2000). 'An Assessment of the Total External Costs of UK Agriculture'. *Agricultural Systems*, 65: 113–36.

Raupp, J. (1994). 'Some Ideas and Guidelines for Research on Ecological Agriculture'. *American Journal of Alternative Agriculture*, 9, 1–2: 84–7.

Röder, E. (2002). 'Biolandbau in Deutschland – Aktuelle Entwicklungen in der Erzeugung und Vermarktung'. Unpublished manuscript, 10 January 2002.

Roosen, J, J. L. Lusk and J. A. Fox (2001). 'Consumer Demand for and Attitudes Toward Alternative Beef Labelling Strategies in France, Germany, and the UK'. In Selected Papers, American Agricultural Economics Association Annual Meeting, Chicago, 5–8 August 2001.

Schaer, B. (2001). 'Regionales Gemeinschaftsmarketing für Öko-Lebensmittel – dargestellt am Beispiel der Konzeption des Zeichens "Öko-Qualität aus Bayern"'. In Öko-Management – Studien zur ökologischen Betriebsführung, Vol. 4, Hamburg: Verlag Kovač.

Schneeberger, W., M. Eder and A. Posch (1997). 'Strukturanalyse der Biobetriebe in Österreich'. Der Förderungsdienst, 45, 12: 1–16 (Special Supplement to Series 12/97). Available from the Internet: <http://www.boku.ac.at/iao/eder/biobetriebe96.> 14 August 2001.

Stolze, M. (1998). 'Organisationsformen ostdeutscher landwirtschaftlicher Großbetriebe nach der Umstellung auf ökologischen Landbau'. Agribusiness and Food, Vol. 2. Bergen/Dumme: AgriMedia.

Stolze, M., A. Piorr, A. Häring and S. Dabbert (2000). 'The Environmental Impact of Organic Farming in Europe'. In Organic Farming in Europe: Economics and Policy, Vol. 6, Stuttgart-Hohenheim: University of Hohenheim.

Tress, B. (2000). Landwirt schafft Landschaft – Umstellungspotential und landschaftliche Konsequenzen der ökologischen Landwirtschaft in Dänemark. Forschungsrapport 121, Roskilde: Universität Roskilde.

Waibel, H. and G. Fleischer (1998). Kosten und Nutzen des chemischen Pflanzenschutzes in der deutschen Landwirtschaft aus gesamtwirtschaftlicher Sicht. Wissenschaftsverlag Vauk KG, Kiel.

Waibel, H. and G. Fleischer (2002). 'Experience with Cost Benefit Studies of Pesticides in Germany'. Paper presented at the OECD workshop on the Economics of Pesticide Reduction in Agriculture, Copenhagen, Denmark, 28–30 November 2001.

Wier, M. and C. Calverley (1999). Forbrug af okologiske fodevarer. Del 1: Den okologiske forbruger. Faglig rapport fra DMU (National Environmental Research Institute), Nr. 272.

Willer, H. and M. Yussefi (2002). Organic Agriculture Worldwide 2002. Statistics and Future Prospects, Stiftung Ökologie und Landbau (SÖL) Special Issue 74.

Woese, K., D. Lang, C. Boess and K. W. Bögl (1995). Ökologisch und konventionell erzeugte Lebensmittel im Vergleich – Eine Literaturstudie. BgVV (Bundesministerium für gesundheitlichen Verbraucherschutz und Veterinärmedizin)–Hefte, Vol. 4. Dahlem.

World Organic News (2002). 'UK's "Big Three" Account for Two out of Three Sales'. No. 59, 5 December 2002.

WTO (2001). 'Trading into the Future: Introduction to the WTO – Agriculture'. Available from the Internet: http://www.wto.org/english/ tratop_e/agric_e/agric_e.htm. 12 December 2001.

Wynen E. and D. Vanzetti (1999). 'Research in Organic Agriculture'. Paper presented at the Organic Farming Conference at ISARA, Lyon.

Yussefi, M. (2001). 'Analyse der Märkte für Lebensmittel aus ökologischem Landbau sowie deren Entwicklungsmöglichkeiten am Beispiel der bedeutendsten außereuropäischen Länder'. Unpublished thesis, Faculty of Agro-Ecology, University of Rostock, February 2001.

Zanoli, R. and D. Gambelli (1999). 'Output and Public Expenditure Implications of the Development of Organic Farming in Europe'. In Organic Farming in Europe: Economics and

Policy, Vol. 4, Stuttgart-Hohenheim: University of Hohenheim.

Zanoli R. and S. Naspetti (2001). 'Values and Ethics in Organic Food Consumption'. In Pasquali M. (ed.), Preprints of the Third Congress of the European Society for Agricultural and Food Ethics: Food Safety, Food Quality, Food Ethics, Florence, 3–5 October 2001, Milan: A & Q.

Zanoli, R., D. Gambelli and D. Vairo (2000). 'Organic Farming in Europe by 2010: Scenarios for the Future'. In *Organic Farming in Europe: Economics and Policy*, Vol. 8, Stuttgart-Hohenheim: University of Hohenheim.

Zanoli, R., D. Vairo and P. Midmore (2001a). 'Literature Review of Existing Consumer-Related Studies Concerning Organic Food in Europe'. Unpublished report, Deliverable D1, EU project (QLK5-2000-01124), 'Organic Marketing Initiatives and Rural Development', Aberystwyth.

Zanoli, R., S. Naspetti and D. Vairo (2001b). 'Organic Products and Consumer Product Knowledge'. Mimeo, University of Ancona.

Zerger, U. (1999). 'Wird die Forschung den Bedürfnissen der Praxis gerecht?' *Ökologie & Landbau* 27, 1: 46–7.

ZMP (Zentrale Markt und Preisberichtstelle für Erzeugnisse der Land-, Forst- und Ernährungswirtschaft) (2001). *Einstellungen und Käuferprofile bei Bio-Lebensmitteln*, Bonn: ZMP.

Organisations with interest in organic farming

International Organisations

IFOAM
c/o Oekozentrum Imsbach
66636 Tholey-Theley
Germany
Tel: +49 6853 919890
Fax: +49 6853 919899
http://www.ifoam.org
headoffice@ifoam.org

Food and Agriculture Organisation of the United Nations (FAO)
Viale delle Terme di Caracalla
00100 Rome
Italy
Tel: +39 06 5705 1
Fax: +39 06 5705 3152
http://www.fao.org
fao-hq@fao.org

Pesticides Action Network (PAN) Europe
Eurolink Centre
49 Effra Road
London SW2 1BZ
UK
Tel: +44 20 7274 8895
Fax: +44 20 7274 9084
http://www.pan-europe.net
coordinator@pan-europe.de

Organic Trade Association
PO Box 547
Greenfield, MA 01302
USA
Tel: 1 413 774 7511
Fax: 1 413 774 6432
http://www.ota.com
info@ota.com

International Trade Centre UNCTAD/WTO (ITC)
Palais des Nations 1211
Geneva 10
Switzerland
Tel: +41 22 730 01 11
Fax : +41 22 733 44 39
http://www.intracen.org
itcreg@intracen.org

Research Organisations

Forschungsring für Biologisch-Dynamische Wirtschaftsweise
Brandschneise 1
64295 Darmstadt
Germany
Tel: +49 6155 84123
Fax: +49 6155 846911
http://www.forschungsring.de
Immo.Luenzer@Forschungsring.de

Forschungsinstitut für biologischen Landbau (FiBL)
Ackerstrasse
5070 Frick
Switzerland
Tel: +41 62 865 72 72
Fax: +41 62 865 72 73
http://www.fibl.ch
admin@fibl.ch
Web-Project:
http://www.organic-europe.net

Louis Bolk Institute
Hoofdstraat 24
3972 LA Driebergen
Netherlands
Tel: +31 343 52 38 60
Fax: +31 343 51 56 11
http://www.louisbolk.nl
info@louisbolk.nl

The Rodale Institute
611 Siegfriedale Road
Kutztown, PA 19530-9320
USA
Tel: +1 610 683 1400
Fax: +1 610 683 8548
http://www.rodaleinstitute.org
info@rodaleinst.org

Ludwig-Boltzmann-Institute for Biological Agriculture and Applied Ecology
Rinnböckstrasse 15
1110 Vienna
Austria
Tel: +43 1 7951 497943
Fax: +43 1 7951 47393
http://www.organic-research.com/research/Projects/DOCEA/inst4.asp

HDRA
Ryton Organic Gardens, Coventry
Warwickshire CV8 3LG
Great Britain
Tel: +44 24 7630 3517
Fax: +44 24 7663 9229
http://www.hdra.org.uk
enquiry@hdra.org.uk

Elm Farm Research Centre
Hamstead Marshall
Newbury RG20 0HR
Great Britain
Tel: +44 1488 658298
Fax: +44 1488 658503
http://www.efrc.com
elmfarm@efrc.com

The Norwegian Centre for Ecological Agriculture
6630 Ingvoll
Norway
Tel: +47 71 53 20 00
Fax: +47 71 53 20 01
http://www.norsok.no
norsok@norsok.no

Danish Research Centre for Organic Farming (DARCOF)
Foulum, P.O. Box 50
8830 Tjele
Denmark
Tel: +45 89 99 10 35
Fax: +45 89 99 16 75
http://www.darcof.dk
foejo@agrsci.dk

Centre for Sustainable Agriculture (CUL)
Box 7047
750 07 Uppsala
Sweden
Tel: +46 18 67 10 00
Fax: +46 18 67 35 71
http://www.cul.slu.se
jessica.alm@cul.slu.se

Institut Technique de l'Agriculture
Biologique (ITAB)
149, rue de Bercy
75595 Paris cedex 12
France
Tel: +33 1 40 04 50 64
Fax: +33 1 40 04 50 66
http://www.itab.asso.fr
itab@itab.asso.fr

Henry A. Wallace Institute for
Alternative Agriculture
9200, Edmonston Road, Suite 117
Greenbelt, Maryland, MD 20770-1551
USA
http://www.hawiaa.org

National Organisations

Austria

ARGE Bio-Landbau
Wickenburggasse 14/9
1080 Wien
Tel: +43 810 221314
Fax: +43 140 27800
http://www.bioinformation.at
service@bioinformation.at

Österreichische Interessensgemeinschaft für
biologische Landwirtschaft (ÖIG)
Hanriederstr. 8/1
4132 Lembach
Austria
Tel: +43 7286 20022
Fax: +43 7286 20033
http://www.oekoland.at
igbiolandbau@oekoland.at

Ernte fuer das Leben
Bio Ernte Austria
Europaplatz 4
4020 Linz
Austria
Tel. +43 732 654 884
Fax +43 732 654 884 40
http://www.bio-ernte.at
bio@ernte.at

Oesterreichischer Demeter-Bund
Hietzinger Kai 127/2/31
1130 Wien
Austria
Tel: +43 1 8794701
Fax: +43 1 8794722
http://www.demeter.at
info@demeter.at

Foerderungsgemeinschaft fuer gesundes
Bauerntum, ORBI
Nöbauerstr. 22
4060 Leonding
Austria
Tel: +43 732 675363

Biolandwirtschaft Ennstal
8950 Stainach 160
Austria
Tel. +43 3623 20116
Fax: +43 03623 20117
http://www.bioland-ennstal.at
office@bioland-ennstal.at

Verein der biologisch wirtschaftenden
Ackerbaubetriebe, BAF
2164 Gut Prerau
Austria
Tel: +43 2523 8412
Fax: +43 2523 8412

Freiland-Verband
Wickenburggasse 14/9
1080 Wien
Austria
Tel. +43 1 408 88 09
Fax +43 1 402 78 00
http://www.freiland.or.at
office@freiland.or.at

Hofmarke – Bioverband
4553 Schlierbach 226
Austria
Tel.: +43 07582 61404-0
Fax.: +43 07582 61404-4
http://www.hofmarke.at
office@hofmarke.at

Bioverband Erde und Saat
Hanriederstrasse 8
4132 Lembach
Austria
Tel.: +43 7286 7517
Fax: +43 7286 7517 20
http://www.erde-saat.de
office@erde-saat.at

Dinatur
Schlag 14
2871 Zöbern
Austria
Tel: +43 2642 8651 19
Fax: +43 2642 8651 9
http://www.dinatur.at
dinatur@nextra.at

**Konsumenten und Produzentenarbeits-
gemeinschaft (KOPRA)**
Hirschgraben 15
6800 Feldkirch
Austria
Tel: +43 5522 79687
Fax: +43 5522 79687 11
http://www2.vol.at/kopra
kopra@verein.vol.at

**Verein organisch-biologischer Landbau
Weinviertel**
Peigarten 52
2053 Peigarten
Austria
Tel: +43 2944 8263
Fax: +43 2944 8402
http://www.oekoland.at/mitglieder/kettler_
unten.html
biohof.kettler@aon.at

**Ökowirt Informationsservice für Bauern
und Konsumenten**
Feyregg 39
4552 Wartberg/Krems
Austria
Tel: +43 7587 7177 12
Fax: +43 7587 7177 29
http://www.oekoland.at/oekowirt
oekowirt@oekoland.at

Bergkräuter-Genossenschaft Sarleinsbach
Thierberg 32
4192 Hirschbach
Austria
Tel: +43 7948 8702
Fax: +43 7948 8702 13
http://www.bergkraeuter.at
groedl@bergkraeuter.at

Biohof-Gemeinschaft Pannonische Region
Wiener Neustädter Str. 34
7032 Sigless
Austria
Tel: +43 2626 71222
Fax: +43 2626 712255

Belgium

BIOFORUM asbl
Leuvensebaan 368
3040 Sint-Agatha-Rode
Belgium
Tel: +32 16 47 01 98
Fax: +32 16 47 01 99
http://www.bioforum.be
info@probila-unitrab.be

BIOFORUM Chambre Wallonne
Rue des Fossés Fleuris 39
5000 Namur
Belgium
Tel: +32 81 83 58 00
Fax: +32 81 83 58 00

Naredi
Zavelput, 7
1000 Brüssel
Belgium
Tel: +32 2 2186760
Fax: +32 2 2186679

Belbior, Vlaamse Beroepsvereniging voor
Biologische Boeren
Statiestraat 164 c
2600 Berchem
Belgium
Tel: +32 3 2873772
Fax: +32 3 2873771
http://www.bioforum.be/belbior.html
wim.vandenberghe@belbior.be

UNAB, Union nationale des
Agrobiologistes Belges
Le Quesniau 14
7870 Montignies-Lez-Lens
Tel: +32 65 227260
Fax: +32 65 227260
http://www.bioforum.be/fr/landbouwer.html
unab@skynet.be

PROBILA-UNITRAB
Leuvensebaan 368
3040 Sint-Agatha-Rode
Tel: +32 16 47 01 98
Fax: +32 016 47 01 99
http://www.probila-unitrab.be
hugo.baert@probila-unitrab.be

Cyprus

Cyprus Organic Producers Association
Apostolos Andreas 14
4607 Pissouri village
Cyprus
Fax: +357 5 221996

Czech Republic

Libera
Vajdova 1/1029
10200 Prag 10
Czech Republic
Tel: +42 2 7922417

Pro Bio
Nemocnicni 53
78701 Sumperk
Czech Republic
Tel: +420 649 216609
Fax: +420 649 214586
http://www.pro-bio.cz
pro-bio@pro-bio.cz

Denmark

Demeterforbundet i Danmark, Forening
for Biodynamisk Jordbrug
Birkum Bygade 20
5220 Odense SOE
Denmark
Tel: +45 6597 3050
Fax: +45 6597 3250
or
Frederiksgade 72
8000 Aarhus C
Tel: +45 86 19 94 45
Fax: +45 65 97 30 50
http://www.okologiens-hus.dk/biodynamisk
biodynamisk-forening@mail.tele.dk

Landsforeningen Oekologisk Jordbrug /
Oekologiens Hus
Danish Association for Organic Farming
Frederiksgade 72
8000 Aarhus
Denmark
Tel: +45 87322700
Fax: +45 87322710
http://www.okologiens-hus.dk

Estonia

Estonian Biodynamic Association
J. V. Jannseni 4
51005 Tartu
Estonia
Tel: +372 7 422 051

Estonian Organic Producers Union
Pärnu mnt. 139 c
11317 Tallinn
Estonia
Tel: +372 6 558 399
Fax: +372 6 558 414
lyrand@hot.ee

Kagu-Eesti Bios
Nomme 2
65603 Voru
Estonia
Tel: +372 5 072 487

Finland

Biodynaaminen yhdistys - Biodynamiska förening
Finnish Biodynamic Association
Uudenmaankatu 25 A 4
00120 Helsinki
Finland
Tel: +358 9 644 160
Fax: +358 9 680 2591
http://www.biodyn.fi
info@biodyn.fi

Ekologiska Odlarna pa Aland
Borgboda
22430 Saltvik, Aland
Finland
Tel: +358 18 43512
Fax: +358 18 43612

The Central Union of Agricultural Producers and Forest Owners (MTK)
P.O.Box 510
Simonkatu 6
00100 Helsinki
Finland
Tel: +358 9 131 151
Fax: +358 9 131 15409
http://www.mtk.fi/english.htm

Union of Organic Farming, Luomo-Liitto
P.O. Box 42
01301 Vantaa
Finland
Tel: +358 9 8570 6600
Fax: +358 9 8570 6601
http://www.luomulehti.luomu-liitto.fi
anu.tuomola@luomu-liitto.fi

France (F)

Fédération Nationale d'Agriculture Biologique (FNAB)
40, rue de Malte
75011 Paris
France
Tel: +33 1 43 38 38 69
Fax: +33 1 43 38 39 70
f.n.a.b@wanadoo.fr

Association Française d'Agriculture Biologique (AFAB)
3, rue de Mourzouk
44300 Nantes
France
Tel: +33 2 40 49 47 90

Mouvement de Culture Bio-Dynamique (Demeter)
5, Place de la Gare
68000 Colmar
France
Tel: +33 3 89 24 36 41
Fax: +33 3 89 24 27 41
http://bio-dynamie.org
info@bio-dynamie.org

Germany

Bund Ökologische Lebensmittelwirtschaft (BÖLW)
Marienstraße 20
10117 Berlin
Germany
Tel. +49 30 28482305
http://www.boelw.de
info@boelw.de

Biokreis e.V.
Regensburger Str. 34
94032 Passau
Germany
Tel: +49 0851 75650 0
Fax: +49 0851 75650 25
http://www.biokreis.de
biokreis@t-online.de

Bioland - Verband für organisch-biologischen Landbau
Kaiserstraße 18
55116 Mainz
Germany
Tel: +49 6131 2 39 79 0
Fax: +49 6131 2 39 79 27
http://www.bioland.de
oeffentlichkeitsarbeit@bioland.de

Biopark
Karl-Liebknecht-Str. 26
19395 Karow
Germany
Tel: +49 38738 70309
Fax:+49 38738 70024
http://www.biopark.de
info@biopark.de

Ecovin - Bundesverband Ökologischer Weinbau
Wormser Str. 162
55276 Oppenheim
Germany
Tel: +49 6133 1640
Fax: +49 6133 1609
http://www.ecovin.de
ecovin@t-online.de

Forschungsring für Biologisch-Dynamische Wirtschaftsweise
Brandschneise 1
64295 Darmstadt
Germany
Tel: +49 6155 84123
Fax: +49 6155 846911
http://www.forschungsring.de
Immo.Luenzer@Forschungsring.de

Gäa - Vereinigung Ökologischer Landbau
Am Beutlerpark 2
01217 Dresden
Germany
Tel: +49 351 40 12 389
Fax: +49 351 40 155 19
http://www.gaea.de
info@gaea.de

Naturland - Verband für naturgemäßen Landbau
Kleinhadernerweg 1
82166 Gräfelfing
Germany
Tel: +49 89 89 80 82 0
Fax: +49 89 89 80 82 90
http://www.naturland.de
naturland@naturland.de

Ökosiegel e.V. - Verein Ökologischer Landbau
Barnser Ring 1
29581 Gerdau
Germany
Tel: +49 5808 1834
Fax: +49 5808 1834

Assoziation Oekologische Lebensmittelhersteller
Zum Pilsterhof 7
97769 Oberleichtersbach
Germany
Tel: +49 9741 4834
Fax: +49 9741 932201

Bundesfachverband der Reformhäuser
Gotische Str. 15
61440 Oberursel
Germany
Tel: +49 6172 3009861
Fax: +49 6172 3009862
http://www.refo.de

Bundesverband Naturkost Naturwaren
Herstellung und Handel eV (BNN)
Ebertplatz 1
50668 Köln
Germany
Tel: +49 221 139 756 44
Fax: +49 139 756 40
http://www.n-bnn.de

Stiftung Ökologie & Landbau (SÖL)
Weinstraße Süd 51
67098 Bad Dürkheim
Germany
Tel: +49 6322 989700
Fax +49 6322 989701
http://www.soel.de
info@soel.de
Web-Project:
http://organic-europe.net

Forschungsinstitut für biologischen Landbau
FiBL Berlin e.V.
Rungestrasse 19
10179 Berlin
Germany
Tel: +49 30 2758175 0
Fax: +49 30 2758175 9
http://www.fibl.de
berlin@fibl.de

Schweisfurth-Stiftung
Südliches Schlossrondell 1
80638 München, Germany
Tel: +49 89 17 95 95 10
Fax: +49 89 17 95 95 19
http://www.schweisfurth.de
cthomas@schweisfurth.de

Zukunftsstiftung Landwirtschaft
Oskar-Hoffmann-Str. 25
44789 Bochum
Germany
Tel: +49 234 5797 141
Fax: +49 234 5797 188
http://www.zs-l.de
info@zs-l.de

Gregor Louis oder Umweltstiftung
Brienner Straße 46
80333 München
Germany
Tel: +49/89/54 21 21 42
Fax: +49/89/52 38 93 35
http://www.umweltstiftung.com
info@umweltstiftung.com

Gesellschaft für ökologische Tierhaltung
(GÖT) e.V.
c/o Fachgebiet Angewandte
Nutztierethologie und Artgemäße
Tierhaltung
Universität GH Kassel (GhK)
Nordbahnhofstr. 1a
372130 Witzenhausen
Germany
Tel. +49 5542 981640
Fax: +49 5542 981588
http://www.goet.de
hoerning@goet.de

Great Britain (UK)

Organic Farmers & Growers Ltd
The Elim Centre, Lancaster Road
Shrewsbury, Shropshire SY1 3LE
Great Britain
Tel: +44 1743 440512
Fax: +44 1743 461441
info@organicfarms.uk.com

Organic Food Federation
The Tithe House, Peaseland Green, Elsing
East Dereham NR20 3DY
Great Britain
Tel: +44 1362 637314
Fax: +44 1362 637398

Scottish Organic Producers Association
Suite 15, Software Centre
Stirling University Innovation Park
Stirling, FK9 4NF
Great Britain
Tel: +44 1786 458090
Fax: +44 1786 458091
http://www.sopa.org.co.uk
contact@sopa.demon.co.uk

Soil Association
Bristol House, 40-56 Victoria Street
Bristol BS1 6BY
Great Britain
Tel: +44 117 929 0661
Fax: +44 117 925 2504
http://www.soilassociation.org
info@soilassociation.org

The Biodynamic Agricultural Association
Painswick Inn Project
Gloucester Street, Stroud
Glos GL5 1QG
Great Britain
Tel: +44 1453 759501
Fax: +44 1453 759501
http://www.anth.org.uk/biodynamic
bdaa@biodynamic.freeserve.co.uk

Greece

Association of Bio-Cultivators of Arcadia
Municipal Centre of the Municipality
22100 Tripoli
Greece
Tel: +30 71 243305
Fax: +30 71 243305

Association of Ecological Agriculture of Greece
Ktima Pyrgou Vassiliasis
10433 Athens
Greece
Tel: +30 1 2387227
Fax: +30 1 2387027

Bioagros - Organic Olive Farmers of Thasos
64002 Limenaria
Greece
Tel: +30 593 51706
Fax: +30 593 51706

CAEG - Cretan Agri-Environmental Group
PO Box 59
70400 Moirae
Greece
Tel: +30 81 32 6589
Fax: +30 892 22026 or +30 892 22828
agapi-v@otenet.gr

Cooperative of Fruit Producers of Velvendos
Velvendos
50400 Kozani
Greece

Dimitra - Association of Bio-Cultivators of Helia
27100 Pyrgos
Greece
Tel: +30 621 71085
Fax: +30 621 33244

DIO
Aristtonikou 23-25
10433 Athens
Greece
Fax: +30 1 9224685
dio@ath.forthnet.gr

EAS Aegalias
25100 Aegio
Greece
Tel: +30 691 25928

EEVE-Union of Organic Farmers of Greece
And. Metaxa 13-15
10681 Athen
Greece
Tel: +30 1 364 7766
Fax: +30 1 330 4647

Farmers' Cooperative of Krokos
Krokos
50010 Kozani
Greece
Tel: +30 461 63283

GAIA Cooperative of Producers and Consumers of Organic Products
Dimokratias 93-95
73100 Chania
Greece
Tel: +30 821 28783

Group of Kiwi Producers of Meliki
Meliki
59031 Alexandria
Greece
Tel: +30 331 81438

Group of Kiwi Producers of Palaios Prodromos
Palaios
59100 Alexandria
Greece
Tel: +30 331 95098

Kefala - Sparti A.E.
Kefalas
23100 Sparti
Greece
Tel: +30 731 77455
Fax: +30 731 81851

PEZA UNION - Peza Agrarian Cooperatives Ass/n of Iraklion Prefecture
Post Box 1077
71110 Iraklion
Greece
Tel: +30 81 741945
Fax: +30 81 741528
http://www.aias.net/peza_union/index.html

Hungary

Biodynamic Association
Eötvös u. 24
7090 Tamási
Hungary
Tel: +36 60 364 469
Fax: +36 23 343 148

Biokultúra
Kitaibel Pál u. 4
1024 Budapest
Hungary
Tel: +36 1 316 2138
Fax: +36 1 316 2139

IFOAM Central Eastern European Regional Group
Bécsi út 211
1032 Budapest
Hungary
Tel: +361 387 8007
Fax:+361 387 8007
fruhwald@mail.datanet.hu

Iceland

The Farmers Association of Iceland
P.O. Box 7080, Baendahöllin
107 Reykjavik
Iceland
Tel: +354 563 0300 / 0317
Fax: +354 562 3058
http://www.bondi.is
ord@bondi.is

VOR - Verndun Og Ræktun, The National Association of Organic Farmers
Akur, Bisk
801 Selfoss
Iceland
Tel: +354 486 8983
Fax: +354 486 8938
akurbisk@isholf.is

Ireland

Bio-Dynamic Agriculture Association of Ireland (BDAAI)
The Watergarden
Thomastown, Co. Kilkenny
Ireland
Tel: +353 56 5 42 14
Fax: +353 56 5 42 14
http://www.kihe.com/demeter
bdaai@indigo.ie

Irish Organic Farmers and Growers Association (IOFGA)
Harbour Building
Harbour Road
Kilbeggan, Co. Westmeath
Ireland
Tel: +353 506 32563
Fax: +353 506 32063
http://irishorganic.ie
gibneyiofga@eircom.net

Organic Trust
Vernon House
2 Vernon Avenue, Clontarf
Dublin 3
Ireland
Tel: +353 1 8530271
Fax: +353 1 8530271
http://www.organic-trust.org
organic@iol.ie

Italy

**AMAB Associazione Mediterranea
Agricoltura Biologica**
Via Po 25/c
00198 Roma
Italy
Tel: +39 06 84497423
Fax: +39 06 84497269
http://www.amab.it
amab@amab.it

**Associazione Italiana per l'Agricoltura
Biologica (AIAB)**
Via Piave 14
00187 Roma
Italy
Tel: +39 06 45437485/6/7
Fax: +39 06 45437469
http://www.aiab.it
aiab@aiab.it

Biozert - Bioland - Südtirol
Steindlweg 48
39018 Terlan
Italy
Tel: +39 471 256977
Fax: +39 471 256062
http://www.bioland-suedtirol.de
bioland@rolmail.net

Coordinamento Toscano Produttori Biologici
Piazza Dalmatia 20/C
50141 Firenze
Italy
Tel: +39 55 413173
Fax: +39 55 413172
ctpb@mclink.it

Il Buratto
Via Colle Rosetta
01033 Civita Castellana
Italy
Tel: +39 0761 54200
Fax: +39 0761 542001
sgratiliano@isa.it

**Pro.B.E.R. - Associazione Produttori
Biologici e Biodinamici Emilia Romagna**
Via Fioravanti, 22
40122 Bologna
Italy
Tel: +39 051 6313374
Fax: +39 051 6313374
http://www.prober.it
prober@prober.it

IFOAM Italy Group
Organic movement
Via dei Tigli 2
33034 Fagagna (UD)
Tel: +39 0432 800 371
Fax: +39 0432 800 371
cddab@iol.it

Liechtenstein

Verein Bio-Liechtenstein
Brühlgasse 539
9492 Eschen
Liechtenstein
Tel: +423-3732302
Fax: +423-3732302

Luxembourg

Bio-Bauerngenossenschaft BioG
161, rue de Rollingergrund
2440 Luxembourg
Luxembourg
Tel: +352 447877
Fax: +352 442432

Saatbaugenossenschaft
4, rue de Bastogne
9706 Clervaux
Luxembourg
Tel: +352 92116726
Fax: +352 921854

Verain fir biologesch-dynamesch Landwirtschaft
13, rue de la Gare
5353 Oetrange
Luxembourg
Tel: +352 355961
Fax: +352 350245
http://www.biokuh.lu

Vereinigung für biologischen Landbau Luxemburg a.s.b.l.
Haus vun der Natur 'Kräizhaff'
route de Bettembourg
1899 Luxembourg
Tel: +352 29 04 04 314
Fax: +352 29 05 04
http://www.biolandbau.lu
secretary@biolandbau.lu

Netherlands

BD-Vereniging -houdster Demeter keurmerk
Diederichslaan 25
3970 AE Driebergen
Netherlands
Tel: +31 343 531740
Fax: +31 343 516943
http://www.demeter-bd.nl
info@demeter-bd.nl

Federatie van Biologische Boeren
c/o Platform Biologica
Nieuwegracht 15
3501 AA Utrecht
Netherlands
Tel: +31 30 2339970
Fax: +31 30 6322989701
http://www.platformbiologica.nl
melita@platformbiologica.nl

Nederlandse Vereniging voor Ekologische Landbouw (NVEL)
Postbus 12048
3501 AA Utrecht
Netherlands
Tel: +31 30 2339970
Fax: +31 30 2304423
http://www.platformbiologica.nl
info@platformbiologica.nl

VB-DB Vereniging van Biologisch-Dynamische Boeren
Nieuwegracht 15
3501 AA Utrecht
Netherlands
Tel: +31 30 2339970
Fax: +31 30 2304423
http://www.platformbiologica.nl
info@platformbiologica.nl

Norway

Biologisk-dynamisk Forening, Biodynamic Society
Kirkegata 64
2609 Lillehammer
Norway
Tel: +47 61 22 39 10
Fax: +47 61 25 46 00
biodynfo@frisurf.no

Norsk Økologisk Urtelag, Norwegian Organic Herb Organisation
Planteforsk Kise
2350 Nes
Norway
Tel: +47 62 35 29 06
Fax: +47 62 35 24 90

Oikos - Økologisk Landslag, Norwegian Association for Organic Agriculture
Postboks
8875 Youngstorget
0028 Oslo
Norway
Tel: +47 22 33 21 31
Fax: +47 85 02 66 63
http://www.oikos.no
info@oikos.no

OkoProdusentane, Organic Producers
P.O. Box 193
2040 Kløfta
Norway
Tel: +47 63 98 18 80
Fax: +47 63 98 18 81
http://home.telia.no/ekoprodusentane
ekoprodusentane@ah.telia.no

Poland

Ekoland – Association of Producers of Organic Food, Stowarzyszenie Producentów Zywnosci Metodami Ekolo
Swiatki k/Szczecinka
78-40 Szczecinek
Poland
Tel: +489 43724395
Fax: +489 43724395
http://free.ngo.pl/ekoland
ekoland4@poczta.onet.pl

Portugal

Agrobio – Associaçao portuguesa de Agricultura Biológica
Calçada da Tapada 39 - r/c D
1300 Lisboa
Portugal
Tel: +351 21 364 13 54
Fax: +351 21 362 35 86
http://www.agrobio.pt
agrobio@mai.teleweb.pt

AJAMPS – Associaçao de Jovens agricultores da Madeira e por
Caminho do Meio
9050 Funchal
Portugal
Tel: +351 291 22 22 75

Bioana
Quinta Pires Marques. Lote 242 - r/c E, Loja B
6000 Castelo Branco
Portugal
Tel: +351 277202950

Salva - Associaçao de Productores em Agricultura Biologica do Sul
Quinta da Figueirinha
8300 -028 Silves
Portugal
Tel: +351 282 44 26 71
Fax: +351 282 44 42 26
http://www.qdf.pt/salva
salva@qdf.pt

Slovenia

Association for Organic Farming for Dolenjska,
Posavje in Bela Krajina,
Zdruzenje za ekolosko kmetovanje
Smihelska 14
8000 Novo mesto
Slovenia

Association for Organic Farming Gorenjska,
Zdruzenje ekoloskih kmetov Gorenjske
Triglavska 12
4264 Bohinjska Bistrica
Slovenia

Association for Organic Farming in Northeast
Slovenia, Zdruzenje za ekolosko kmetovanje
SV Slovenije
Vinarska 14
2000 Maribor
Slovenia
Tel: +386 62 228 490
Fax: +386 62 219 482

Organic Farmers Association Coast Region,
Zdruzenje ekoloskih kmetov Obale
Larisova 7
6280 Ankaran
Slovenia

Organic Producers and Processors Association
'Deteljica', Zdruzenje ekoloskih pridelovalcev
Trnoveljska 1
3000 Celje
Slovenia
Tel: +386 63 425 550

Slovenian Organic Farmers Associations
(S.O.F.A.), Zdruzenje ekoloskih kmetov
Slovenije
Metelkova 6
1000 Ljubljana
Slovenia
Tel: +386 41 725 991
Fax: +386 61 1337 029
ekokmet@attglobal.net

Society for biodynamic husbandry
'AJDA', Drustvo za biolosko-dinamicno
gospodarjenje 'AJDA'
Vrzdenec 60
1354 Horjul
Slovenia
Tel: +386 1 7540743
Fax: +386 1 7540751
ajda.sloveija@siol.net

Union of Slovenian Organic Farmers
Associations, Zveza zdruzenj ekoloskih
kmetov Slovenije
Metelkova 6
1000 Ljubljana
Slovenia
Tel: +386 1 4397460
Fax: +386 1 4397105
http://www.zveza-ekokmet.si
zveza.ekokmet@zveza-ekokmet.si

Spain

Asociación de Agricultura Biodinámica de
España
Can Ricastell
08399 Tordera
Spain
Tel: +34 93 7650380
Fax: +34 93 7641784

Asociación Vida Sana
Clot 39, 2, bajos
08018 Barcelona
Spain
Tel: +34 3 5800818
Fax: +34 3 5801120
http://www.vidasana.org
info@vidasana.org

FA-B
Bonavista, 15, 2, 4e
08012 Barcelona, Spain
Tel: +34 93 4157184
Fax: +34 93 4153170
fa-bio@retemail.es

Sociedad Espanola de Agricultura
Ecologica - SEAE (Spanish society for
ecological agriculture)
Granja La Peira. Apdo 107
46450 Benifaió, Valencia, Spain
Tel: +34 96 178 80 60
Fax: +34 96 178 81 62
http://www.agroecologia.net/
seaeseae@worldonline.es

Sweden

Biodynamiska föreningen, The Swedish Biodynamic Association
Skillebyholm
15391 Järna
Sweden
Tel: +46 8 551 579 88
Fax: +46 8 551 579 76
http://www.demeter.nu
info@demeter.nu

Ekologiska Lantbrukarna i Sverige, Swedish Ecological Farmers Association
Sågargatan 10 A
75318 Uppsala
Sweden
Tel: +46 18 10 10 06
Fax: +46 18 10 10 66
http://www.ekolantbruk.se
kansliet@ekolantbruk.se

Förbundet Organisk Biologisk Odling, FOBO, Association of Organic Biological Growers
St. Jörgens Väg 20
42249 Hisings Backa
Sweden
Tel: +46 31 1050740
Fax: +46 31 55 68 81
http://www.fobo.nu
anders.lund@ekocentrum.nu

Switzerland

Bio Suisse
Margarethenstrasse 87
4053 Basel
Switzerland
Tel: +41 61 3859610
Fax: +41 61 3859611
http://www.bio-suisse.ch
bio@bio-suisse.ch

Biovin, Schweizerischer Bioweinbauverein
101, rte de Mandement
1242 Satigny
Switzerland
Tel: +41 22 753 40 31
Fax: +41 22 753 40 23
biovin@worldcom.ch

Verein für biologisch-dynamische Landwirtschaft
Grabenackerstr. 15 / Postfach 761
4142 Münchenstein
Switzerland
Tel: +41 61 4160643
Fax: +41 61 4160644
http.//www.demeter.net
kuefferheer@dplanet.ch

Vereinigung für biologischen Kräuteranbau im Schweizer Berggebiet
Hillenberg
8636 Wald
Switzerland

Bioterra Schweiz - Gesellschaft für biologischen Landbau
Dubsstr. 33
8003 Zürich
Switzerland
Tel: +41 1 463 55 14
Fax: +41 1 463 48 49
http://www.bioterrra.ch
ueli.affolter@bioterra.ch

Index

cooperatives 63, 81
Copenhagen Declaration 97-9
criticism of organic farming 82-4
Czech Republic 102

Danish Research Centre (DARCOF)
37, 39, 41
Denmark 5, 10, 17-18, 22-4, 26, 28, 31,
37, 41, 44, 46, 50, 55-9, 77, 97-8,
102, 111, 122, 125, 136; National
Council for Organic Farming 57-8
Doha 111

education 39-42, 128, 133; see also
information, training
Elm Farm Research Centre (EFRC)
(UK) 37, 39
employment/unemployment 2, 76, 79-
81, 87, 97, 105, 115
energy conservation 69
environmental degradation 1-2, 92,
108
environmentalism, 4-5, 7, 20-1, 32-4,
36, 39, 43-6, 58, 60, 64, 66-71, 73,
81, 83, 89-90, 93-9, 101-2, 105-6,
108-9, 112-19, 121, 125-7, 131,
133, 135, 138
Estonia 102
Europe, Eastern 92, 102, 124, 137;
Central 92, 102, 124, 137;
Northern 21; Western 1, 106, 124
European Action Plan 98-101, 136-7
European Council on Agriculture 97,
99-100
European Union (EU), AIR and
FAIR research programmes 32-3;
Commission 29, 74-5, 92, 94-100,
104-5, 111, 131; Council 102; and
developing countries 101; enlargement of 3, 92-3, 102-6, 111, 113,
124; food quality/safety in 75-6;
organic farming expands in 2, 5, 9-

13, 55-65; organic farming legislation in 2-3, 5-6, 42-54, 56, 58-62,
71, 75, 88-9, 94, 96-7, 99, 104, 110,
114, 122, 128. 130, 134, 137-8;
organic farming lobby in 29;
organic farming origins in 4; as
world standard for organic farming
130; and the WTO 94, 96, 106-11
exports 18, 48, 55, 58, 62, 106, 111,
137
extension work 40, 128
externalities 71-2

famine 93
farming incomes 66, 76-8, 81, 87, 90,
92-3, 95, 98, 116
FDB 56
feedstuffs 13
fertilisers, and biodiversity 68; in
extensive agriculture 13; as external
input 33; and funding (lack of) for
organic farming 41, 133; low-
intensity use 96; McSharry Reform
and 43; reduction in (effects
estimated) 72-3; and technological
change in agriculture 1-2
Finland 10,17, 28, 31, 37, 44, 46, 55,
77
Fischler, Commissioner 100
Food and Agricultural Organisation
(FAO) 3
food distribution/marketing 25-7, 46-7,
55, 64, 79, 81, 88, 94, 101, 106,
115-16, 118-19, 121-2, 126, 128,
130-1
food prices 1, 22-5, 45-8, 55-6, 77, 83-
5, 92-3, 113-14, 116-19, 121, 123,
126, 132
food processing 25, 27, 46-7, 50, 52,
55, 64,79, 81, 94, 106, 115-16, 119,
121, 127-8, 131
food quality 34, 66, 73-6, 88, 95, 99,

Zed Books titles on agriculture

Jerry Buckland
Ploughing Up the Farm
Neoliberalism, Modern Technology
and the State of the World's Farmers
1 84277 366 6 Hb
1 84277 367 4 Pb

Patricia L. Howard (ed.)
Women and Plants
Gender Relations in Biodiversity
Management and Conservation
1 84277 156 6 Hb
1 84277 157 4 Pb

John Madeley
Food for All
The Need for a New Agriculture
1 84277 018 7 Hb
1 84277 019 5 Pb

Helena Norberg-Hodge, Peter
Goering and John Page
From the Ground Up
Rethinking Industrial Agriculture
– Revised Edition
1 85649 993 6 Hb
1 85649 994 4 Pb

Helena Norberg-Hodge, Todd
Merrifield and Steven Gorelick
Bringing the Food Economy Home
Local Alternatives to Global
Agribusiness
1 84277 232 5 Hb
1 84277 233 3 Pb

Stephen Nottingham
Genescapes
The Ecology of Genetic Engineering
1 84277 036 5 Hb
1 84277 037 3 Pb

Stephen Nottingham
Eat Your Genes
How Genetically Modified Food Is
Entering Our Diet
– New Updated Edition
1 84277 346 1 Hb
1 84277 347 X Pb

Helena Paul and Ricarda
Steinbrecher, with Devlin Kuyek
and Lucy Michaels
Hungry Corporations
Transnational Biotech Companies
Colonise the Food Chain
1 84277 300 3 Hb
1 84277 301 1 Pb

Robert Ali Brac de la Perrière
and Franck Seuret
Brave New Seeds
The Threat of GM Crops to Farmers
1 85649 899 9 Hb
1 85649 900 6 Pb

Brian Tokar (ed.)
Redesigning Life? The Worldwide
Challenge to Genetic Engineering
1 85649 834 4 Hb
1 85649 835 2 Pb

For full details about these titles and Zed's general and subject
catalogues, please write to: The Marketing Department, Zed Books,
7 Cynthia Street, London N1 9JF, UK
or e-mail Sales@zedbooks.demon.co.uk

Visit our website at: http://www.zedbooks.co.uk